The C++ Programming Bible: From Basics to Advanced Concepts

A Step-by-Step Guide to Building Complex Applications with C++

BOOZMAN RICHARD

BOOKER BLUNT

Table of Content

TABLE OF CONTENTS

INTRODUCTION

The C++ Programming Bible: From Basics to Advanced Concepts

C++ is one of the most powerful and widely used programming languages in the world. It is the backbone of many performance-critical systems that require fine-grained control over system resources. From video games to high-performance computing, from mobile applications to large-scale enterprise systems, C++ is a language that empowers developers to create efficient, high-quality software. However, with its immense capabilities comes complexity. Understanding how to harness the full potential of C++ requires mastery over both its foundational principles and its more advanced features.

This book, **"The C++ Programming Bible: From Basics to Advanced Concepts,"** is designed to guide you through every aspect of C++ programming, from the basics to the most advanced techniques. Whether you are a beginner who has never written a line of code or an experienced developer looking to deepen your knowledge, this book offers a comprehensive roadmap to mastering C++.

C++ is known for its speed, efficiency, and control over system resources. It is used in a wide range of applications that require high performance, such as video games, operating systems, and embedded systems. With the rise of new technologies like artificial intelligence, blockchain, and IoT (Internet of Things), C++ continues to be a relevant and powerful language. However, to fully understand its capabilities, developers must learn not only how to write efficient code but also how to manage memory, optimize performance, and apply modern C++ features in real-world scenarios.

This book is divided into **27 comprehensive chapters**, each focusing on a key aspect of C++ programming. The chapters are designed to provide you with a strong foundation and gradually build your knowledge, preparing you to tackle complex, real-world challenges in software development. Whether you are learning how to manage memory efficiently, implement object-oriented principles, or optimize performance in high-performance applications, this book will provide you with the tools and knowledge to excel.

The Structure of the Book

The book is structured in a logical progression, starting with the fundamentals of C++ and building up to more advanced topics. Here's a glimpse of how the book is organized:

1. **Chapters 1-3** lay the groundwork for beginners, introducing the basics of C++ syntax, control structures, and functions. These chapters ensure that you have a strong understanding of how C++ code works and how to use basic features like variables, loops, and conditionals.

2. **Chapters 4-6** dive into object-oriented programming (OOP) concepts. You will learn about classes, objects, inheritance, polymorphism, and abstraction—key principles that form the backbone of modern C++ applications. These chapters focus on writing clean, reusable, and modular code using OOP principles.

3. **Chapters 7-9** introduce more advanced C++ features such as the Standard Template Library (STL), memory management, and templates. You'll learn how to use the powerful data structures provided by the STL and how to optimize memory usage in performance-critical applications.

4. **Chapters 10-12** tackle exception handling, file I/O, and string manipulation—crucial aspects of building

robust, real-world applications. You will learn how to handle errors gracefully, read and write data from files, and manipulate text data effectively.

5. **Chapters 13-16** explore concurrency and multithreading, working with game engines, and developing real-time systems. These chapters are especially relevant for building high-performance applications that require parallel processing or real-time performance.

6. **Chapters 17-21** cover critical advanced topics like algorithms, design patterns, and C++ in modern tech. You will explore concepts like time complexity, Big-O notation, and learn how to apply C++ in fields like artificial intelligence (AI), blockchain development, and high-performance computing.

7. **Chapters 22-24** provide practical guidance on working with embedded systems, IoT, and optimizing code for performance. These chapters are designed to show you how C++ can be applied in low-level programming and real-time systems, as well as how to fine-tune your code for maximum efficiency.

8. **Chapters 25-27** bring everything together, offering insights into the future of C++ and concluding with

best practices, tips for mastering the language, and exploring its evolving role in modern technology.

Real-World Applications of C++

While learning the theory behind C++ is crucial, this book also emphasizes **practical, real-world applications**. Throughout the chapters, you will encounter real-world examples and case studies that demonstrate how C++ can be used to solve complex problems across various domains.

- **Game Development**: C++ is the primary language used in building AAA video games and interactive simulations. The book explores game engines like **Unreal Engine** and demonstrates how C++ can be used to create high-performance games with advanced graphics, physics, and AI.
- **Embedded Systems and IoT**: C++ is extensively used in embedded systems and IoT applications, where efficiency and resource management are critical. In this book, you'll learn how to program microcontrollers, interact with sensors, and build devices that interact with the real world.

- **High-Performance Computing (HPC)**: C++ plays a central role in scientific simulations, financial modeling, and complex computational problems that require massive computational power. The book covers how to optimize C++ code for performance and utilize parallel computing techniques.

- **Blockchain and AI**: C++ has a strong presence in blockchain development, with major cryptocurrencies like **Bitcoin** and **Ethereum** being written in C++. Additionally, the book explores C++'s growing role in AI and machine learning, especially in performance-critical tasks such as deep learning model training and inference.

Mastering C++: Tips and Resources

The path to mastering C++ is challenging but highly rewarding. This book provides several strategies to help you along the way:

1. **Practice Regularly**: C++ is a language that requires continuous practice. Writing code, solving problems,

and building projects are the best ways to reinforce your knowledge.

2. **Embrace Modern C++**: As C++ evolves, new features are introduced that make the language more powerful and safer. Keep up with the latest C++ standards (C++11, C++14, C++17, and C++20) to take advantage of modern features like smart pointers, lambda expressions, and range-based algorithms.

3. **Leverage Libraries and Tools**: C++ has a vast ecosystem of libraries and tools that can make development easier and more efficient. The book introduces you to popular libraries like **Boost, Qt, OpenGL**, and more, helping you build powerful applications faster.

4. **Participate in the Community**: The C++ community is large and active, with resources available through forums, blogs, and open-source projects. Participating in these communities can help you learn from others and stay updated on best practices.

Conclusion

"The C++ Programming Bible: From Basics to Advanced Concepts" is a comprehensive guide designed to help you become proficient in C++. Whether you're just starting or looking to deepen your understanding, this book covers the language from all angles, including foundational concepts, advanced techniques, and real-world applications. By following the principles and examples laid out in this book, you'll be equipped to tackle complex software projects, optimize code for performance, and use C++ in cutting-edge fields like game development, AI, IoT, and blockchain.

C++ is not just a language—it's a powerful tool that allows developers to push the boundaries of what's possible in software. As you work through this book, you will gain the skills to leverage the full power of C++ and use it to create efficient, scalable, and high-performance applications that meet the demands of the modern tech landscape. Happy coding!

CHAPTER 1

INTRODUCTION TO C++ PROGRAMMING

Overview of C++: History, Importance, and How It Evolved

C++ is one of the most powerful and widely used programming languages, known for its efficiency, flexibility, and ability to handle complex systems and applications. Developed by **Bjarne Stroustrup** in **1979** at Bell Labs, C++ began as an enhancement to the C programming language, initially aimed at providing object-oriented programming (OOP) capabilities. C++, sometimes referred to as "C with classes," merged procedural programming with object-oriented features to offer a more robust framework for creating scalable and high-performance applications.

C++'s Evolution:

- **1979-1980s:** Initially, C++ was a small experimental project designed to add object-oriented features to the C programming language. It was called "C with Classes." The concept of classes and objects, which allowed the bundling of data and methods, was a significant step forward.

- **1985:** C++ was officially released, complete with the Standard Template Library (STL), which enabled developers to utilize containers and algorithms for better code efficiency.

- **1990s and Beyond:** Over the years, C++ continued to evolve, with updates like C++98, C++11, and more recently, C++14 and C++17, introducing advanced features such as **smart pointers, move semantics, lambdas**, and **multithreading capabilities**. The most recent version, **C++20**, brings even more features such as **concepts**, **ranges**, and **coroutines**, making C++ a modern, multi-paradigm programming language.

- **Importance of C++ Today:** C++ remains one of the most popular and versatile programming languages due to its ability to run highly optimized code, which makes it a go-to for **system programming, game development, embedded systems**, and **high-performance applications**. From operating systems and browsers to video games and embedded systems, C++ powers numerous applications across industries.

Setting Up the Development Environment: How to Install and Configure IDEs like Visual Studio, Code::Blocks, or CLion

Before you can start writing and running your C++ programs, you'll need to set up a development environment on your computer. Here, we will guide you through setting up an IDE (Integrated Development Environment) for C++ development. There are several options available, with **Visual Studio**, **Code::Blocks**, and **CLion** being the most popular choices for beginners and advanced developers.

1. Visual Studio:

Visual Studio is a powerful IDE for Windows users that supports C++ and many other programming languages. It provides a feature-rich interface with tools for debugging, profiling, and testing.

- **Steps for Installation:**
    1. Go to the Visual Studio website.
    2. Download the free **Community Edition**.
    3. During installation, ensure you select the **Desktop development with C++** workload.
    4. Once installed, launch Visual Studio, and you're ready to start coding!
- **Why Choose Visual Studio?** It's known for its user-friendly interface, excellent debugging tools, and

integration with Microsoft's suite of development tools. It also offers extensive support for **Windows application development**.

2. Code::Blocks:

Code::Blocks is a free, open-source IDE that works across multiple platforms (Windows, Linux, macOS). It's lightweight and easy to use, making it a great option for beginners.

- **Steps for Installation:**
    1. Go to the Code::Blocks website.
    2. Download the **installer with MinGW** (this comes with the necessary compiler).
    3. Follow the installation prompts and launch the IDE once installed.
- **Why Choose Code::Blocks?** It's a straightforward IDE with support for **multiple compilers** and is ideal for users who prefer an open-source environment without extra bloat.

3. CLion:

CLion, developed by JetBrains, is another excellent IDE that is particularly known for its C++ support. It provides advanced features like **code refactoring**, **smart code completion**, and **integration with version control systems**.

- **Steps for Installation:**
    1. Visit the CLion website.
    2. Download and install the software (CLion offers a 30-day free trial).
    3. After installation, configure your **compiler** and **debugger** (CLion integrates seamlessly with **GCC**, **Clang**, or **MSVC**).
- **Why Choose CLion?** CLion is particularly useful for developers who want advanced features like **refactoring tools, built-in testing frameworks, and easy integration with version control systems**.

Your First C++ Program: Writing a Simple "Hello, World!" Program

Once you've set up your development environment, it's time to write your first C++ program! In this chapter, we'll walk through writing a basic **Hello, World!** program, which is a common starting point for learning any new programming language.

cpp

```
#include <iostream>  // Include the input/output
stream library

int main() {
    std::cout << "Hello, World!" << std::endl;
// Output the text to the console
```

19

```
    return 0;   // Indicate that the program ended
successfully
}
```

Let's break down the key parts of the program:

1. **#include <iostream>:** This line tells the compiler to include the **input/output stream** library, which is required for input and output operations (like printing to the console).

2. **int main()**: This is the main function where your program begins. Every C++ program must have a `main` function, and it's where execution starts.

3. **std::cout << "Hello, World!" << std::endl;:** This line prints the text **"Hello, World!"** to the console. The << operator is used to send output to the console, and `std::endl` moves the cursor to the next line after printing.

4. **return 0;:** This indicates that the program has run successfully and is returning control to the operating system.

Real-World Example: "Hello, World!" in a Small Desktop App

Now that we've learned how to print "Hello, World!" to the console, let's build a simple desktop application that demonstrates the same functionality, but with a graphical interface. For this, we'll use **Qt**, a popular framework for creating cross-platform desktop apps in C++.

Here's how to set up a basic window with a button that, when clicked, prints "Hello, World!" to the console.

1. **Install Qt:** First, install **Qt** by visiting Qt's website and following the installation instructions.
2. **Create a New Project:** Open Qt Creator, create a new project, and choose **Qt Widgets Application**.
3. **Write the Code:** Replace the content of `mainwindow.ui` and `mainwindow.cpp` with the following code:

mainwindow.cpp:

cpp

```cpp
#include "mainwindow.h"
#include "ui_mainwindow.h"
#include <QPushButton>
#include <QMessageBox>

MainWindow::MainWindow(QWidget *parent) :
    QMainWindow(parent),
    ui(new Ui::MainWindow)
{
    ui->setupUi(this);
```

```
    // Create a button
    QPushButton *button = new QPushButton("Click
Me", this);
    button->resize(200, 100);    // Resize the
button
    button->move(100, 100);    // Move the button
to the center of the window

    // Connect the button click to a function
    connect(button, &QPushButton::clicked, this,
&MainWindow::showMessage);
}

MainWindow::~MainWindow()
{
    delete ui;
}

void MainWindow::showMessage() {
    // Show a message box with Hello, World!
    QMessageBox::information(this,    "Message",
"Hello, World!");
}
```

Explanation:

- This code creates a simple window with a **QPushButton** labeled "Click Me." When the button is clicked, a

QMessageBox is displayed, showing the message "Hello, World!"

- This real-world example introduces the **Qt** library, which is widely used for building C++ applications with graphical user interfaces.

By the end of this chapter, you'll have learned how to:

1. Set up your development environment for C++.
2. Write a basic C++ program that prints "Hello, World!" to the console.
3. Expand on this knowledge to create a simple desktop application with a graphical interface using Qt.

In the next chapter, we'll dive deeper into C++ syntax, control structures, and fundamental programming concepts.

CHAPTER 2

BASICS OF C++ SYNTAX AND STRUCTURE

Variables and Data Types: Overview of Built-in Types, Constants, and Data Type Conversions

In C++, **variables** are used to store data, and each variable must be declared with a specific **data type**. The data type defines what kind of data the variable can hold and the amount of memory it requires.

Built-in Data Types in C++

C++ offers a variety of built-in data types, which can be categorized as follows:

1. **Integral Types** (used to store integers):
   - `int`: A basic integer type, typically 4 bytes in size, used for whole numbers.
   - `short`: A shorter integer type, usually 2 bytes.
   - `long`: A larger integer type, typically 4 or 8 bytes.

o **long long**: Even larger integers, typically 8 bytes.

2. **Floating-point Types** (used for real numbers):

   o **float**: Single-precision floating point (4 bytes).

   o **double**: Double-precision floating point (8 bytes).

   o **long double**: Extended precision floating point (usually 10 or 12 bytes).

3. **Character Types** (used for characters and text):

   o **char**: Stores a single character (1 byte).

   o **wchar_t**: A wide character type (usually 2 or 4 bytes), used for international characters.

4. **Boolean Type** (used for true/false values):

   o **bool**: Can hold one of two values: **true** or **false**.

5. **Void Type** (used when no value is required):

   o **void**: Used for functions that don't return a value.

Constants

Constants are values that cannot be changed during program execution. In C++, constants can be defined using the **const** keyword.

Example:

cpp

```
const int MAX_AGE = 120;  // MAX_AGE is a constant
integer value
```

Data Type Conversions

In C++, **type casting** or **type conversion** is used to convert one data type to another. There are two types of conversions:

- **Implicit Conversion** (done automatically by the compiler):
    - Happens when there's no risk of data loss.
    - Example: Converting from `int` to `float` automatically.
- **Explicit Conversion** (done manually by the programmer):
    - Done using **casting operators** like `static_cast`, `dynamic_cast`, or C-style cast.
    - Example:

cpp

```
int a = 10;
double b = static_cast<double>(a);    //
Explicit conversion from int to double
```

Operators: Arithmetic, Relational, Logical, and Bitwise Operators

Operators in C++ are symbols used to perform operations on variables and values. C++ supports a wide variety of operators.

Arithmetic Operators

Used for basic mathematical operations:

- **+** (Addition)
- **-** (Subtraction)
- ***** (Multiplication)
- **/** (Division)
- **%** (Modulus, returns the remainder of division)

Example:

cpp

```
int a = 10, b = 3;
int sum = a + b;      // sum = 13
int remainder = a % b;  // remainder = 1
```

Relational Operators

Used to compare two values:

- **==** (Equal to)
- **!=** (Not equal to)

- **>** (Greater than)
- **<** (Less than)
- **>=** (Greater than or equal to)
- **<=** (Less than or equal to)

Example:

cpp

```cpp
int a = 10, b = 3;
bool isEqual = (a == b);  // isEqual = false
bool isGreater = (a > b);  // isGreater = true
```

Logical Operators

Used to perform logical operations:

- **&&** (Logical AND)
- **||** (Logical OR)
- **!** (Logical NOT)

Example:

cpp

```cpp
bool x = true, y = false;
bool result = (x && y);  // result = false (AND
operation)
```

Bitwise Operators

Used to manipulate individual bits of data:

- **&** (AND)
- **|** (OR)
- **^** (XOR)
- **~** (NOT)
- **<<** (Left shift)
- **>>** (Right shift)

Example:

cpp

```
int a = 5, b = 3;  // a = 0101, b = 0011
int result = a & b;  // result = 1 (0001)
```

Input and Output (I/O): Using cin and cout for User Interaction

C++ provides simple mechanisms to handle input and output using the **cin** and **cout** streams.

Using cin for Input

The cin stream is used to receive input from the user. It is typically used with the **>>** operator.

Example:

cpp

```cpp
int age;
std::cout << "Enter your age: ";  // Ask the user
for input
std::cin >> age;  // Take user input and store it
in the variable 'age'
```

Using cout for Output

The cout stream is used to display output to the console. It is used with the **<<** operator.

Example:

cpp

```cpp
std::cout << "Your age is " << age << std::endl;
// Output the value of 'age' to the console
```

Combining cin and cout

You can combine both cin and cout to create interactive programs where you ask for user input and then display results:

Example:

cpp

```cpp
#include <iostream>
int main() {
    int num1, num2;
    std::cout << "Enter two numbers: ";    // Prompt the user
    std::cin >> num1 >> num2;  // Take input
    int sum = num1 + num2;  // Calculate sum
    std::cout << "The sum is: " << sum << std::endl;  // Output the result
    return 0;
}
```

Real-World Example: A Simple Calculator for Basic Arithmetic Operations

Let's now put these concepts together by creating a simple calculator program. The program will allow the user to input two numbers and then perform basic arithmetic operations like addition, subtraction, multiplication, and division.

Here's the code:

```cpp
cpp

#include <iostream>
using namespace std;

int main() {
```

```cpp
    double num1, num2;
    char operation;

    // Ask the user for input
    cout << "Enter first number: ";
    cin >> num1;

    cout << "Enter operator (+, -, *, /): ";
    cin >> operation;

    cout << "Enter second number: ";
    cin >> num2;

    // Perform the calculation based on the
operator
    if (operation == '+') {
        cout << "Result: " << num1 + num2 << endl;
    }
    else if (operation == '-') {
        cout << "Result: " << num1 - num2 << endl;
    }
    else if (operation == '*') {
        cout << "Result: " << num1 * num2 << endl;
    }
    else if (operation == '/') {
        if (num2 != 0) {
            cout << "Result: " << num1 / num2 <<
endl;
        }
```

```
    else {
        cout << "Error! Division by zero." <<
endl;
    }
}
else {
    cout << "Invalid operator!" << endl;
}

return 0;
}
```

Explanation:

1. **Input:** The program prompts the user to enter two numbers and an operator.

2. **Arithmetic Operations:** It checks which operator the user entered and performs the corresponding arithmetic operation.

3. **Error Handling:** If the user attempts to divide by zero, the program displays an error message.

4. **Output:** Finally, it displays the result of the calculation.

By the end of this chapter, you will have a solid understanding of:

- Basic data types and constants in C++.
- How to perform calculations using various operators.

- How to take input and display output using `cin` and `cout`.
- Implementing these concepts in a **simple calculator program** that can be expanded with more features later on.

In the next chapter, we will explore **Control Structures and Flow**—which includes conditional statements and loops, building on the foundational knowledge you've learned here.

CHAPTER 3

CONTROL STRUCTURES AND FLOW

Conditional Statements: if, else, and switch

Conditional statements in C++ allow you to execute specific blocks of code depending on whether a condition is **true** or **false**. These are the foundation for decision-making in programming.

The if Statement

The if statement evaluates a condition and executes a block of code if the condition is **true**.

Example:

cpp

```
int score = 75;
if (score >= 50) {
    std::cout << "You passed the exam!" <<
std::endl;
}
```

- In the above example, the condition score >= 50 is checked. If **true**, the message "You passed the exam!" is displayed.

The else Statement

The else statement is used when the if condition evaluates to **false**. It defines an alternative block of code that gets executed when the condition is not met.

Example:

cpp

```
int score = 45;
if (score >= 50) {
    std::cout << "You passed the exam!" <<
std::endl;
} else {
    std::cout << "You failed the exam. Try
again!" << std::endl;
}
```

- In this case, the message "You failed the exam. Try again!" is displayed because the condition score >= 50 is **false**.

The switch Statement

The switch statement is useful when you have multiple possible conditions and want to execute a specific block of code based on the value of a variable. It's often more readable than using multiple if-else statements.

Example:

cpp

```
int day = 3;
switch (day) {
    case 1: std::cout << "Monday" << std::endl;
break;
    case 2: std::cout << "Tuesday" << std::endl;
break;
    case 3: std::cout << "Wednesday" <<
std::endl; break;
    default: std::cout << "Invalid day" <<
std::endl; break;
}
```

- Here, the value of day is compared to the case values. If day equals 3, it will print "Wednesday". The break statement is used to exit the switch block after executing the matched case.

Loops: `for,` `while,` *and* `do-while` *Loops*

Loops allow you to repeat a block of code multiple times, making your program more efficient and reducing redundancy.

The `for` Loop

The `for` loop is commonly used when you know beforehand how many times you want to repeat a block of code. It's ideal for iterating over a sequence of values, such as numbers in a range.

Example:

cpp

```cpp
for (int i = 0; i < 5; i++) {
    std::cout << "Iteration number: " << i << std::endl;
}
```

- The `for` loop starts by initializing `i` to 0, checks if `i` < 5, and increments `i` after each iteration. The loop will run 5 times, printing the iteration number each time.

The `while` Loop

The `while` loop runs as long as the condition is **true**. It's typically used when you don't know how many iterations you need in advance.

Example:

cpp

```
int i = 0;
while (i < 5) {
    std::cout << "Iteration number: " << i <<
std::endl;
    i++;
}
```

- The `while` loop will continue running as long as i < 5. After each iteration, i is incremented.

The do-while Loop

The `do-while` loop is similar to the `while` loop, but it guarantees that the block of code is executed at least once, even if the condition is **false**.

Example:

cpp

```
int i = 0;
do {
    std::cout << "Iteration number: " << i <<
std::endl;
    i++;
```

```
} while (i < 5);
```

- Here, the code will always run at least once before checking if i < 5.

Break and Continue Statements

In some cases, you may want to alter the normal flow of a loop. **break** and **continue** statements are used to exit or skip iterations within a loop, respectively.

The break Statement

The break statement is used to exit the loop completely, even if the loop's condition is still true.

Example:

cpp

```cpp
for (int i = 0; i < 10; i++) {
    if (i == 5) {
        break;  // Exit the loop when i equals 5
    }
    std::cout << "Iteration number: " << i <<
std::endl;
}
```

- This loop will print the iteration numbers from 0 to 4, and then the break statement will stop the loop when i equals 5.

The continue Statement

The continue statement skips the current iteration of the loop and proceeds with the next iteration.

Example:

cpp

```cpp
for (int i = 0; i < 5; i++) {
    if (i == 2) {
        continue;  // Skip the iteration when i
equals 2
    }
    std::cout << "Iteration number: " << i <<
std::endl;
}
```

- This loop will print iteration numbers 0, 1, 3, and 4, skipping the iteration where i equals 2.

Real-World Example: A Program to Grade Student Scores and Display Results Based on Conditions

Let's apply what we've learned to create a program that grades student scores and displays results based on the conditions provided. The program will ask for the student's score, then determine the grade based on predefined thresholds, and finally display the grade.

cpp

```cpp
#include <iostream>
using namespace std;

int main() {
    int score;

    // Ask the user for the student's score
    cout << "Enter the student's score: ";
    cin >> score;

    // Grade the student based on the score
    if (score >= 90) {
        cout << "Grade: A" << endl;
    }
    else if (score >= 80) {
        cout << "Grade: B" << endl;
    }
    else if (score >= 70) {
```

```
        cout << "Grade: C" << endl;
    }
    else if (score >= 60) {
        cout << "Grade: D" << endl;
    }
    else {
        cout << "Grade: F" << endl;
    }

    // Bonus: Check if the student passed or
failed
    if (score >= 60) {
        cout << "Status: Passed" << endl;
    } else {
        cout << "Status: Failed" << endl;
    }

    return 0;
}
```

Explanation:

1. The program asks the user to enter the student's score.

2. It then uses **if-else if-else** statements to determine the grade based on the score.

3. The program further checks whether the student passed or failed by evaluating if the score is greater than or equal to 60.

4. The result is displayed on the console.

By the end of this chapter, you will have a solid understanding of:

- **Conditional statements** like `if`, `else`, and `switch` to make decisions in your code.
- How to **loop** through operations using `for`, `while`, and `do-while` loops.
- The use of **break** and **continue** to control the flow of loops.
- A practical example of **grading student scores** and displaying results using conditional logic.

In the next chapter, we'll explore **Functions in C++**, diving deeper into how to organize your code into reusable blocks for better maintainability and structure.

CHAPTER 4

FUNCTIONS IN C++

Function Declaration and Definition

In C++, functions allow you to organize and reuse code, making your programs more modular and easier to maintain. A function is a block of code that performs a specific task and can be executed when called.

Function Declaration

A **function declaration** (also called a function prototype) tells the compiler about the function's name, return type, and parameters (if any) before its actual definition. It allows the compiler to know about the function before it's used in the program.

Syntax:

cpp

```
return_type function_name(parameter_list);
```

Example:

cpp

```
int add(int a, int b);  // Function declaration
```

Here, int is the return type, add is the function name, and it takes two parameters of type int.

Function Definition

The **function definition** provides the body of the function, specifying what the function does when called.

Syntax:

cpp

```
return_type function_name(parameter_list) {
    // Function body
}
```

Example:

cpp

```
int add(int a, int b) {
    return a + b;  // Adds a and b, then returns
the result
}
```

In this case, the function add takes two integers as input, adds them together, and returns the sum.

Example: Function Declaration and Definition

cpp

```
#include <iostream>
using namespace std;

int multiply(int x, int y);   // Declaration

int main() {
    int result = multiply(5, 3);   // Function
call
    cout << "The result is: " << result << endl;
    return 0;
}

// Definition of the multiply function
int multiply(int x, int y) {
    return x * y;
}
```

Passing Arguments by Value and Reference

In C++, you can pass arguments to functions in two main ways:

Passing by Value

When you pass an argument by value, a of the actual data is made, and changes to the parameter inside the function do not affect the original argument outside the function.

Example:

cpp

```cpp
void modifyValue(int x) {
    x = 100;   // This change does not affect the
original argument
}

int main() {
    int a = 10;
    modifyValue(a);
    cout << "a = " << a << endl;   // Outputs: a
= 10, because 'a' was not modified
    return 0;
}
```

Passing by Reference

When you pass an argument by reference, the function operates directly on the original data, not on a . Changes made to the parameter inside the function will affect the original argument outside the function.

Example:

cpp

```cpp
void modifyValue(int &x) {
    x = 100;  // This change affects the original argument
}

int main() {
    int a = 10;
    modifyValue(a);
    cout << "a = " << a << endl;  // Outputs: a = 100, because 'a' was modified
    return 0;
}
```

- In this case, since we use the **reference operator (&)** in the function parameter, the original a is modified.

Return Types and Recursion

Return Types

A function in C++ can return a value of any data type (e.g., int, float, char, void if no value is returned). The return type is specified in the function declaration and definition.

Example:

49

cpp

```
int add(int a, int b) {
    return a + b;   // Returns the sum of a and b
}
```

In this example, the function `add` returns an `int`, which is the result of adding `a` and `b`.

Recursion

Recursion is when a function calls itself in order to solve a problem. Recursive functions generally have a base case (a stopping condition) to prevent infinite recursion.

Key Concepts:

- **Base Case**: A condition that stops the recursion.
- **Recursive Case**: The part of the function that calls itself to solve smaller instances of the problem.

Example: Factorial Function The **factorial** of a number `n` is defined as:

- `n! = n * (n-1) * (n-2) * ... * 1` for `n > 0`
- `0! = 1` (base case)

Using recursion, we can define the factorial as:

- factorial(n) = n * factorial(n-1).

Example of a recursive factorial function in C++:

cpp

```cpp
#include <iostream>
using namespace std;

int factorial(int n) {
    // Base case: factorial of 0 is 1
    if (n == 0) {
        return 1;
    } else {
        // Recursive case: n! = n * (n-1)!
        return n * factorial(n - 1);
    }
}

int main() {
    int num;
    cout << "Enter a number to calculate its factorial: ";
    cin >> num;

    cout << "Factorial of " << num << " is: " << factorial(num) << endl;
    return 0;
}
```

Explanation of the Recursive Factorial Function:

1. **Base Case:** When `n == 0`, the function returns 1, as `0!
   = 1`.

2. **Recursive Case:** Otherwise, the function returns `n *
   factorial(n - 1)`. This process continues until `n`
   reaches 0.

3. **Call Stack:** Each recursive call adds a new layer to the
   function call stack, which is resolved when the base case
   is met.

**Real-World Example: Solving Mathematical Problems Using
Recursion**

- Recursive algorithms are used in many real-world
  problems, such as traversing file systems, generating
  permutations, and solving problems like **Fibonacci
  sequences**, **binary search**, and **sorting algorithms** like
  quick sort and **merge sort**.

---

*Real-World Example: A Recursive Factorial Function and Solving
Mathematical Problems*

Let's consider a more practical use of recursion with a
mathematical problem—calculating the **Fibonacci sequence**. The
Fibonacci sequence is a series of numbers in which each number

is the sum of the two preceding ones, typically starting with 0 and 1.

The Fibonacci sequence is defined as:

- $F(0) = 0$
- $F(1) = 1$
- $F(n) = F(n-1) + F(n-2)$ for n > 1.

We can solve this problem using a recursive function.

Example: Fibonacci Sequence in C++:

cpp

```cpp
#include <iostream>
using namespace std;

int fibonacci(int n) {
    if (n <= 1) {
        return n;   // Base cases: F(0) = 0, F(1)
= 1
    } else {
        return fibonacci(n - 1) + fibonacci(n -
2);  // Recursive case
    }
}

int main() {
```

```
    int num;
    cout << "Enter a number to calculate its
Fibonacci value: ";
    cin >> num;

    cout << "Fibonacci value at position " << num
<< " is: " << fibonacci(num) << endl;
    return 0;
}
```

Explanation of the Fibonacci Function:

- **Base Case:** If n is 0 or 1, return n (F(0) = 0, F(1) = 1).
- **Recursive Case:** For n > 1, return the sum of the two previous Fibonacci numbers, `fibonacci(n - 1)` and `fibonacci(n - 2)`.

This recursive function calculates the **nth** Fibonacci number, but keep in mind that it's inefficient for large values of n due to redundant calculations. In real-world applications, iterative solutions or memoization techniques are often used to optimize performance.

Summary:

By the end of this chapter, you should be comfortable with:

- **Function Declaration and Definition**: Understanding how to declare and define functions in C++.

- **Passing Arguments by Value and Reference**: Knowing how data is passed to functions and how to modify original data using references.

- **Return Types and Recursion**: Understanding how to return values from functions and using recursion to solve problems like factorial and Fibonacci.

- **Practical Examples**: Implementing recursive functions and using them in mathematical problems.

In the next chapter, we will dive into **C++ Standard Library (STL)**, exploring its powerful built-in data structures and algorithms that simplify common programming tasks.

CHAPTER 5

OBJECT-ORIENTED PROGRAMMING (OOP) BASICS

Introduction to OOP Concepts: Classes and Objects, Encapsulation, Inheritance, and Polymorphism

Object-Oriented Programming (OOP) is a programming paradigm that organizes software design around **objects**, which are instances of **classes**. This approach makes it easier to structure complex programs and manage large codebases by modeling real-world entities in the code.

1. Classes and Objects

- **Class**: A class is a blueprint or template for creating objects. It defines the properties (attributes) and behaviors (methods) that the objects created from the class will have.
- **Object**: An object is an instance of a class. It represents a real-world entity, and each object has its own unique data but shares the same structure and behaviors defined by the class.

Example:

cpp

```cpp
class Car {
    public:
        string model;
        int year;

        void start() {
            cout << "Car is starting" << endl;
        }
};
```

Here, `Car` is a class that has attributes (`model` and `year`) and a behavior (`start()` method). An object of the `Car` class can be created, and its attributes and behaviors will be specific to that object.

2. Encapsulation

- **Encapsulation** is the concept of bundling the data (attributes) and the methods (functions) that operate on the data into a single unit, the **class**. It also involves restricting direct access to some of an object's components, which is done using **access modifiers** (e.g., `public`, `private`, `protected`).

- This hides the internal state of an object and allows controlled access through methods, improving security and reducing complexity.

Example:

cpp

```
class Car {
    private:
        int speed;   // Private attribute

    public:
        void setSpeed(int s) {   // Public setter
method
            speed = s;
        }

        int getSpeed() {  // Public getter method
            return speed;
        }
};
```

In this example, the speed attribute is **private**, meaning it cannot be directly accessed from outside the class. Access to the speed attribute is controlled through the public methods setSpeed() and getSpeed().

3. Inheritance

- **Inheritance** allows one class to inherit properties and behaviors (methods) from another class, promoting **reusability** and **extensibility**.
- The class that inherits is called the **derived class**, and the class being inherited from is the **base class**.

Example:

cpp

```cpp
class Vehicle {
    public:
        string brand;

        void honk() {
            cout << "Vehicle honking" << endl;
        }
};

class Car : public Vehicle {  // Car is a derived
class
    public:
        string model;
};

int main() {
    Car car1;
```

```
car1.brand = "Toyota";
car1.model = "Corolla";
car1.honk();  // Inherited from Vehicle class
return 0;
}
```

In this case, `Car` inherits from `Vehicle`, meaning it has access to the `brand` attribute and the `honk()` method from the `Vehicle` class.

4. Polymorphism

- **Polymorphism** allows objects of different classes to be treated as objects of a common base class, typically through method overriding or method overloading.
- **Method Overloading**: Same method name with different parameter types.
- **Method Overriding**: Redefining a method in a derived class that has already been defined in the base class.

Example:

cpp

```
class Animal {
    public:
        virtual void sound() {   // Virtual
function for polymorphism
            cout << "Animal sound" << endl;
```

```
        }
};

class Dog : public Animal {
    public:
        void sound() override {    // Overriding
the base class method
            cout << "Bark" << endl;
        }
};

int main() {
    Animal *animal = new Dog();
    animal->sound();    // Outputs "Bark" due to
polymorphism
    return 0;
}
```

Here, the sound() method is **overridden** in the Dog class, and the **virtual keyword** ensures that the appropriate method is called based on the object's type (even if it's referenced through a base class pointer).

Defining Classes and Objects

In C++, defining a class involves specifying the attributes and methods that the class will have. Once the class is defined, you can create objects from it.

61

Class Syntax

cpp

```
class ClassName {
    private:
        // Private attributes and methods

    public:
        // Public attributes and methods
};
```

Example of defining a class with attributes and methods:

cpp

```
class Rectangle {
    private:
        double length, width;

    public:
        // Constructor
        Rectangle(double l, double w) {
            length = l;
            width = w;
        }

        // Method to calculate the area
        double area() {
            return length * width;
        }
```

};

Creating an Object from the Class

Once the class is defined, you can create objects (instances of the class).

Example:

cpp

```
int main() {
    Rectangle rect1(5.0, 3.0);   // Creating an
object with constructor
    cout << "Area of rectangle: " << rect1.area()
<< endl;
    return 0;
}
```

Here, rect1 is an object of type Rectangle, and its area() method is used to calculate the area of the rectangle.

Constructors and Destructors

Constructor

A **constructor** is a special function in a class that is called automatically when an object of that class is created. It initializes the object's attributes and sets up the initial state.

- A constructor has the same name as the class.
- Constructors can take parameters (parameterized constructors) or be without parameters (default constructors).

Example:

cpp

```cpp
class Car {
    public:
        string model;
        int year;

        // Default constructor
        Car() {
            model = "Unknown";
            year = 0;
        }

        // Parameterized constructor
        Car(string m, int y) {
            model = m;
            year = y;
        }
};
```

Destructor

A **destructor** is a special function that is called when an object goes out of scope (i.e., when the object is destroyed). It is used to release resources, such as memory or file handles, that were allocated for the object.

- A destructor has the same name as the class but is preceded by a tilde (~).
- C++ handles the destruction of objects automatically using destructors.

Example:

cpp

```
class Car {
    public:
        string model;

        // Constructor
        Car(string m) {
            model = m;
            cout << "Car " << model << "
created!" << endl;
        }

        // Destructor
        ~Car() {
```

```
        cout << "Car " << model << "
destroyed!" << endl;
        }
};
```

Real-World Example: Modeling Real-Life Objects Like a Car Class with Attributes and Behaviors

Let's create a class that models a real-world object—a **Car**. This class will have attributes such as model and year, and behaviors like start() and stop().

Example:

cpp

```cpp
#include <iostream>
using namespace std;

class Car {
    private:
        string model;
        int year;

    public:
        // Constructor to initialize Car object
        Car(string m, int y) {
            model = m;
```

```cpp
        year = y;
    }


    // Method to start the car
    void start() {
        cout << "The " << model << " is
starting." << endl;
    }


    // Method to stop the car
    void stop() {
        cout << "The " << model << " has
stopped." << endl;
    }


    // Method to display car details
    void display() {
        cout << "Model: " << model << ",
Year: " << year << endl;
    }
};


int main() {
    // Create Car object
    Car myCar("Toyota Corolla", 2020);

    // Access car methods
    myCar.display();
    myCar.start();
```

```
    myCar.stop();

    return 0;
}
```

Explanation:

1. **Attributes:** The `Car` class has two private attributes: `model` and `year`.
2. **Constructor:** The constructor initializes these attributes when the object is created.
3. **Methods:** `start()`, `stop()`, and `display()` provide behaviors and output relevant information about the car.

Summary:

By the end of this chapter, you should have a solid understanding of:

- The **fundamental concepts of Object-Oriented Programming**: classes, objects, encapsulation, inheritance, and polymorphism.
- How to **define and use classes** in C++.
- The role of **constructors and destructors** in managing objects.

- A **real-world example** where we modeled a car using OOP concepts.

In the next chapter, we will explore the **C++ Standard Library (STL)**, learning about useful containers and algorithms that simplify many common programming tasks.

CHAPTER 6

ADVANCED OBJECT-ORIENTED CONCEPTS

Inheritance and Derived Classes

Inheritance is a fundamental feature in **Object-Oriented Programming (OOP)** that allows one class to **inherit** the properties and behaviors of another class. The class that inherits is called the **derived class**, and the class from which it inherits is called the **base class**.

Inheritance allows you to create new classes based on existing ones, promoting **code reuse** and **extensibility**. It is often referred to as a **"is-a"** relationship.

Syntax of Inheritance

In C++, inheritance is implemented by using the **colon (:)** operator, where the derived class is specified after the base class.

Example:

cpp

```cpp
#include <iostream>
using namespace std;

class Animal {
public:
    void eat() {
        cout << "This animal eats food." << endl;
    }
};

class Dog : public Animal {   // Inherits from
Animal
public:
    void bark() {
        cout << "The dog barks!" << endl;
    }
};

int main() {
    Dog dog;
    dog.eat();   // Inherited method
    dog.bark();   // Derived class method
    return 0;
}
```

Explanation:

- `Dog` inherits from `Animal`. The `Dog` class has access to the `eat()` method from the `Animal` class, while also defining its own `bark()` method.
- The `public` keyword means that the inherited members are accessible to the derived class and outside the class as well.

Types of Inheritance:

- **Single Inheritance:** A class inherits from one base class.
- **Multiple Inheritance:** A class inherits from more than one base class.
- **Multilevel Inheritance:** A class is derived from another derived class.
- **Hierarchical Inheritance:** Multiple classes inherit from a single base class.
- **Hybrid Inheritance:** A combination of multiple types of inheritance.

Polymorphism: Method Overloading and Overriding

Polymorphism allows you to use a single interface for different types of objects. It is a key feature of OOP, as it enables **method overriding** and **method overloading**, which provide flexibility and extensibility in your programs.

1. Method Overloading

Method overloading is a feature that allows you to define multiple methods with the same name but different parameter lists. The correct method is chosen based on the number or types of parameters passed when the method is called.

Example:

cpp

```cpp
#include <iostream>
using namespace std;

class Calculator {
public:
    // Overloaded add function
    int add(int a, int b) {
        return a + b;
    }

    double add(double a, double b) {
        return a + b;
    }
};

int main() {
    Calculator calc;
```

```cpp
    cout << "Sum of integers: " << calc.add(3, 4)
<< endl;
    cout << "Sum of doubles: " << calc.add(3.5,
4.5) << endl;
    return 0;
}
```

Explanation:

- In this example, the `add` function is overloaded to accept both `int` and `double` types. The appropriate version of the method is called based on the argument types.

2. Method Overriding

Method overriding occurs when a derived class provides a specific implementation of a method that is already defined in its base class. The base class method is marked with the `virtual` keyword, and the derived class method overrides it with its own implementation.

Example:

cpp

```cpp
#include <iostream>
using namespace std;

class Animal {
```

```cpp
public:
    virtual void sound() {  // Virtual method in
base class
        cout << "Animal makes a sound" << endl;
    }
};

class Dog : public Animal {
public:
    void sound() override {  // Overridden method
in derived class
        cout << "Dog barks" << endl;
    }
};

int main() {
    Animal* animal = new Dog();
    animal->sound();  // Outputs "Dog barks"
    delete animal;
    return 0;
}
```

Explanation:

- The sound() method in the Animal class is **virtual**, allowing the derived class Dog to override it. The program calls the overridden version of the method, demonstrating **runtime polymorphism**.

Abstraction and Interfaces

Abstraction is the concept of **hiding the complex implementation details** of a system and exposing only the necessary functionality. It helps in reducing complexity by providing a simplified interface to the user.

In C++, abstraction is achieved through **abstract classes** and **pure virtual functions**.

Abstract Classes and Pure Virtual Functions

An **abstract class** is a class that cannot be instantiated directly and may contain **pure virtual functions**. A pure virtual function is a function declared in an abstract class that has no implementation in the class itself, forcing derived classes to provide an implementation.

- **Pure Virtual Function Syntax:**

cpp

```
virtual return_type function_name() = 0;
```

Example:

cpp

```cpp
#include <iostream>
using namespace std;

class Shape {
public:
    virtual void draw() = 0;   // Pure virtual
function
};

class Circle : public Shape {
public:
    void draw() override {
        cout << "Drawing a Circle" << endl;
    }
};

class Square : public Shape {
public:
    void draw() override {
        cout << "Drawing a Square" << endl;
    }
};

int main() {
    Shape* shape1 = new Circle();
    Shape* shape2 = new Square();
    shape1->draw();   // Outputs "Drawing a
Circle"
```

```
    shape2->draw();      // Outputs "Drawing a
Square"
    delete shape1;
    delete shape2;
    return 0;
}
```

Explanation:

- `Shape` is an abstract class with a pure virtual function `draw()`. The `Circle` and `Square` classes provide their own implementation of `draw()`.
- You cannot create an object of `Shape` directly, but you can use a pointer of type `Shape` to refer to objects of derived classes, showcasing **polymorphism**.

Real-World Example: Building a Basic Banking System with Classes for Accounts, Transactions, and Customers

Let's now put these advanced OOP concepts into practice by building a basic **banking system**. We will model the system with three key classes: `Account`, `Transaction`, and `Customer`.

Account Class:

The Account class will store information about the bank account, such as the account balance and methods for depositing and withdrawing money.

cpp

```cpp
#include <iostream>
#include <vector>
using namespace std;

class Account {
private:
    int accountNumber;
    double balance;

public:
    Account(int accNum, double initBalance) {
        accountNumber = accNum;
        balance = initBalance;
    }

    void deposit(double amount) {
        balance += amount;
        cout << "Deposited " << amount << ", New
Balance: " << balance << endl;
    }
```

```cpp
    void withdraw(double amount) {
        if (balance >= amount) {
            balance -= amount;
            cout << "Withdrew " << amount << ",
New Balance: " << balance << endl;
        } else {
            cout << "Insufficient balance!" <<
endl;
        }
    }

    double getBalance() {
        return balance;
    }
};
```

Transaction Class:

The `Transaction` class will store information about a transaction and execute deposit or withdrawal operations on an account.

cpp

```cpp
class Transaction {
public:
    static void processDeposit(Account& acc,
double amount) {
        acc.deposit(amount);
    }
```

```cpp
    static void processWithdrawal(Account& acc,
double amount) {
        acc.withdraw(amount);
    }
};
```

Customer Class:

The Customer class will represent a bank customer, storing their information and associated accounts.

cpp

```cpp
class Customer {
private:
    string name;
    vector<Account> accounts;

public:
    Customer(string customerName) {
        name = customerName;
    }

    void    addAccount(int    accNum,    double
initBalance) {
        accounts.push_back(Account(accNum,
initBalance));
    }
```

```cpp
    void displayAccounts() {
        cout << name << "'s Accounts:" << endl;
        for (Account& acc : accounts) {
            cout << "Account Number: " <<
acc.getBalance() << ", Balance: " <<
acc.getBalance() << endl;
        }
    }
};
```

Main Program:

cpp

```cpp
int main() {
    Customer customer1("John Doe");

    // Add two accounts for the customer
    customer1.addAccount(101, 500.00);
    customer1.addAccount(102, 1000.00);

    // Perform transactions

Transaction::processDeposit(customer1.accounts[
0], 200.00);

Transaction::processWithdrawal(customer1.accoun
ts[1], 150.00);

    // Display customer accounts and balances
    customer1.displayAccounts();
```

```
    return 0;
}
```

Explanation:

- The `Account` class models the bank account and has methods to **deposit** and **withdraw** money.
- The `Transaction` class provides static methods to process deposits and withdrawals.
- The `Customer` class stores the customer's information and their accounts, and provides a method to display the accounts.
- The **main function** simulates creating a customer with two accounts, processing transactions, and displaying account information.

Summary:

By the end of this chapter, you should be able to:

- Understand and apply **inheritance** to create derived classes that extend the functionality of base classes.
- Use **polymorphism** to create flexible, reusable code through method overloading and overriding.

- Implement **abstraction** using abstract classes and pure virtual functions to define interfaces.
- Build a **real-world banking system** using these advanced OOP concepts, modeling accounts, transactions, and customers.

In the next chapter, we will explore the **C++ Standard Library (STL)**, which provides useful containers and algorithms to help you manage data more efficiently and write cleaner code.

CHAPTER 7

C++ STANDARD LIBRARY (STL) INTRODUCTION

What is the Standard Library?

The **C++ Standard Library (STL)** is a collection of classes and functions that provide common programming tasks like handling data structures, performing input/output (I/O) operations, and performing algorithms like sorting, searching, etc. The STL is a powerful and flexible part of C++ that allows you to avoid reinventing the wheel and instead focus on the core logic of your application.

The key features of the STL include:

- **Containers**: Data structures that store objects.
- **Algorithms**: Functions that perform operations on containers (like sorting, searching, etc.).
- **Iterators**: Objects used to access and traverse elements in containers.
- **Function objects**: Objects that can be invoked as if they were functions, used mainly in STL algorithms.

The STL helps in writing efficient and maintainable code by providing well-optimized, pre-written classes and functions.

Using the STL for Efficient Programming

The STL is designed to handle tasks that would otherwise require you to write custom implementations of data structures and algorithms. By using the STL, you can improve productivity and focus on more complex logic in your programs. Here's why the STL is important:

- **Efficient Memory Usage**: Containers in the STL are optimized for space and time complexity.
- **Pre-built Algorithms**: You can apply algorithms (like searching, sorting, etc.) to containers without having to implement them yourself.
- **Flexibility**: STL containers work with any data type, and their functionality can be customized to fit your needs.

The STL is particularly useful for tasks that require dynamic memory management, fast access to data, or complex data processing, making it indispensable in modern C++ programming.

Introduction to Common STL Containers: Vectors, Arrays, Maps, and Sets

C++ provides several **containers** in the STL to store and manipulate data. Below, we will explore some of the most commonly used containers: **vectors**, **arrays**, **maps**, and **sets**.

1. Vectors

A **vector** is a dynamic array that can grow and shrink in size. Vectors provide random access to elements, and their size can be adjusted at runtime.

- **Key Features**:
    - **Dynamic sizing**: Vectors automatically resize themselves as elements are added or removed.
    - **Efficient access**: Access elements via indexing.
    - **Random access**: Provides fast access to elements via iterators or indices.

Example:

cpp

```
#include <iostream>
#include <vector>
using namespace std;
```

```cpp
int main() {
    vector<int> vec;   // Declaring a vector of
integers

    // Adding elements
    vec.push_back(10);
    vec.push_back(20);
    vec.push_back(30);

    // Accessing elements
    cout << "First element: " << vec[0] << endl;
    cout << "Second element: " << vec[1] << endl;

    // Iterating over vector
    for (int i : vec) {
        cout << i << " ";
    }
    cout << endl;

    return 0;
}
```

2. Arrays

An **array** in C++ is a fixed-size container that stores elements of the same data type. Unlike vectors, arrays have a fixed size that cannot be changed at runtime.

- **Key Features**:

- o **Fixed size**: Once the array size is defined, it cannot be resized.
- o **Fast access**: Elements can be accessed using an index.

Example:

cpp

```cpp
#include <iostream>
using namespace std;

int main() {
    int arr[] = {10, 20, 30, 40, 50};   // Array
with 5 elements

    // Accessing elements
    cout << "First element: " << arr[0] << endl;
    cout << "Second element: " << arr[1] << endl;

    // Iterating over array
    for (int i = 0; i < 5; i++) {
        cout << arr[i] << " ";
    }
    cout << endl;

    return 0;
}
```

3. Maps

A **map** is a container that stores data in key-value pairs. It is implemented as a balanced binary search tree (usually a Red-Black tree) and provides **logarithmic time complexity** for insertions, deletions, and lookups.

- **Key Features**:
    - o **Unique keys**: Each key can only appear once in a map.
    - o **Efficient lookups**: You can search for values based on their key in logarithmic time.
    - o **Ordered by key**: Maps are always ordered based on their keys.

Example:

cpp

```cpp
#include <iostream>
#include <map>
using namespace std;

int main() {
    map<string, int> studentGrades;

    // Inserting key-value pairs
    studentGrades["Alice"] = 90;
    studentGrades["Bob"] = 85;
```

```cpp
studentGrades["Charlie"] = 88;

// Accessing values
cout << "Alice's grade: " << studentGrades["Alice"] << endl;

// Iterating over map
for (auto& pair : studentGrades) {
    cout << pair.first << ": " << pair.second << endl;
}

return 0;
}
```

4. Sets

A **set** is a container that stores unique elements in no particular order. It is typically used to ensure that each element appears only once in the collection.

- **Key Features**:
    - **Unique elements**: Sets automatically handle duplicates by not allowing them.
    - **Efficient insertion and lookup**: Like maps, sets are implemented as balanced binary search trees.

Example:

cpp

```cpp
#include <iostream>
#include <set>
using namespace std;

int main() {
    set<int> uniqueNumbers;

    // Inserting elements
    uniqueNumbers.insert(10);
    uniqueNumbers.insert(20);
    uniqueNumbers.insert(10);        //  Duplicate,
won't be added

    // Accessing elements
    cout << "Elements in set: ";
    for (int num : uniqueNumbers) {
        cout << num << " ";
    }
    cout << endl;

    return 0;
}
```

Real-World Example: A To-Do List Application Using STL Containers

Now that we've introduced some common STL containers, let's build a **simple to-do list application** using these containers. We'll use a `vector` to store tasks, a `map` to store task IDs and descriptions, and a `set` to manage completed tasks.

To-Do List Program:

cpp

```cpp
#include <iostream>
#include <vector>
#include <map>
#include <set>
using namespace std;

class TodoList {
private:
    map<int, string> tasks;    // Task ID and
description
    set<int> completedTasks;    // Set to store
completed task IDs

public:
    // Add a task
    void addTask(int id, string task) {
        tasks[id] = task;
    }
```

```cpp
    // Mark a task as completed
    void completeTask(int id) {
        if (tasks.find(id) != tasks.end()) {
            completedTasks.insert(id);
            cout << "Task " << id << " marked as
completed: " << tasks[id] << endl;
        } else {
            cout << "Task not found!" << endl;
        }
    }

    // Display all tasks
    void displayTasks() {
        cout << "To-Do List:" << endl;
        for (auto& task : tasks) {
            cout << "Task ID: " << task.first <<
" - " << task.second;
            if (completedTasks.find(task.first)
!= completedTasks.end()) {
                cout << " [Completed]";
            }
            cout << endl;
        }
    }
};

int main() {
    TodoList myList;
```

```cpp
    // Adding tasks
    myList.addTask(1, "Buy groceries");
    myList.addTask(2, "Complete homework");
    myList.addTask(3, "Call the bank");

    // Display tasks
    myList.displayTasks();

    // Completing tasks
    myList.completeTask(2);   // Mark task 2 as
completed

    // Display tasks again
    myList.displayTasks();

    return 0;
}
```

Explanation:

- The `TodoList` class has a `map` to store tasks, with task IDs as keys and descriptions as values.

- The `set` container is used to keep track of completed tasks, ensuring that each task can only be marked as completed once.

- The `addTask` method adds a new task, while `completeTask` marks a task as completed.

- The `displayTasks` method shows the current list of tasks and their completion status.

Summary:

By the end of this chapter, you should:

- Understand the **C++ Standard Library (STL)** and its importance for efficient programming.
- Be familiar with common STL containers like **vectors**, **arrays**, **maps**, and **sets** and understand when to use each.
- Have created a **real-world application** (a to-do list) using these containers.

In the next chapter, we will dive deeper into **advanced STL algorithms** and **iterators**, providing even more tools to make your programming tasks easier and more efficient.

CHAPTER 8

MEMORY MANAGEMENT IN C++

Dynamic Memory Allocation: new, delete, *and Memory Leak Prevention*

In C++, dynamic memory allocation allows programs to allocate memory during runtime. This is essential for creating flexible data structures like dynamic arrays, linked lists, and trees. Dynamic memory is allocated from the **heap** (also called free store), which is managed by the operating system.

1. new Operator:

The new operator is used to allocate memory dynamically. It requests memory from the heap and returns a pointer to the allocated memory.

Example:

cpp

```
int* ptr = new int;   // Allocates memory for one
integer
*ptr = 10;                // Assign value to the
allocated memory
```

```
cout << *ptr << endl;   // Outputs: 10
delete ptr;             // Deallocates the memory
```

- In the example above, memory is allocated for one integer using `new`. The pointer `ptr` holds the address of the allocated memory.
- `delete` is used to free the memory once it's no longer needed.

2. `delete` Operator:

The `delete` operator is used to deallocate memory that was previously allocated with `new`. Using `delete` ensures that memory is returned to the heap and prevents **memory leaks**.

Example:

cpp

```
int* ptr = new int;
delete ptr;   // Properly deallocates the memory
```

3. Memory Leaks:

A **memory leak** occurs when memory is allocated dynamically but is not properly deallocated. This results in memory that is no longer in use but still allocated, leading to inefficient memory usage and eventually causing your program to run out of memory.

Common Causes of Memory Leaks:

- Forgetting to call `delete` after memory is allocated with `new`.
- Losing the pointer to the allocated memory (e.g., by reassigning the pointer without deleting the original memory).

Memory Leak Prevention: To prevent memory leaks:

- Always ensure that `delete` is called after you're done using dynamically allocated memory.
- Consider using **smart pointers** (e.g., `std::unique_ptr`, `std::shared_ptr`) provided by C++11 and later versions to automate memory management and avoid manual `new`/`delete`.

Pointers and References

In C++, pointers and references are used to manage and manipulate data indirectly. Understanding how to use them properly is crucial for efficient memory management.

Pointers:

A **pointer** is a variable that stores the memory address of another variable. Pointers are used for dynamic memory allocation, arrays, and working with data structures like linked lists.

- **Declaring a Pointer:**

cpp

```
int* ptr;   // Declares a pointer to an integer
```

- **Dereferencing a Pointer:** Dereferencing a pointer means accessing the value stored at the memory address the pointer points to.

cpp

```
int x = 10;
int* ptr = &x;  // Pointer holds address of x
cout << *ptr << endl;  // Dereferencing the pointer to get the value of x (outputs: 10)
```

- **Pointer to Dynamically Allocated Memory:**

cpp

```
int* ptr = new int;    // Allocating memory
for one integer
*ptr = 50;             // Assigning a value
to the dynamically allocated memory
delete ptr;            // Deallocating memory
```

References:

A **reference** is an alias for an existing variable. Unlike a pointer, a reference must be initialized when it is declared and cannot be reassigned to refer to a different object once initialized.

- **Declaring a Reference:**

cpp

```
int x = 10;
int& ref = x;  // ref is a reference to x
cout << ref << endl;  // Outputs: 10
```

- **Passing by Reference:** When a function receives a reference as an argument, it can modify the original value passed, unlike passing by value, where the original value is not modified.

cpp

```
void increment(int& num) {
    num++;
}
```

```cpp
int main() {
    int x = 5;
    increment(x);   // Pass by reference
    cout << x << endl;   // Outputs: 6
    return 0;
}
```

Memory Management Functions

C++ provides several functions to manage memory, including allocating and deallocating memory on the heap.

1. new[] and delete[] Operators:

- new[] is used to allocate an array dynamically.
- delete[] is used to deallocate memory allocated with new[].

Example:

cpp

```cpp
int* arr = new int[5];   // Allocating an array of
5 integers
arr[0] = 10;
arr[1] = 20;
```

```
delete[] arr;  // Deallocating the array
```
2. `malloc` and `free` (C-style):

In addition to `new` and `delete`, C++ also supports **C-style memory allocation** using `malloc` and `free`. However, it is recommended to use `new` and `delete` in C++ for better memory management and safety.

- `malloc(size_t size)` allocates raw memory.
- `free(void* ptr)` deallocates memory allocated by `malloc`.

Example:

cpp

```
#include <cstdlib>  // For malloc and free

int* arr = (int*)malloc(5 * sizeof(int));  // Allocating memory for an array of 5 integers
arr[0] = 10;

free(arr);  // Deallocating memory
```

While `malloc` and `free` are valid, using `new` and `delete` is recommended for dynamic memory management in C++.

Real-World Example: Building a Simple Dynamic Array that Resizes as Elements are Added

Let's now build a simple dynamic array that resizes as elements are added. This example will illustrate how to use dynamic memory allocation in C++.

cpp

```cpp
#include <iostream>
using namespace std;

class DynamicArray {
private:
    int* arr;
    int size;
    int capacity;

public:
    DynamicArray(int initCapacity = 2) {
        capacity = initCapacity;
        arr = new int[capacity];    // Allocate
memory for the array
        size = 0;
    }

    void addElement(int element) {
        // Resize the array if needed
        if (size == capacity) {
```

```
            capacity  *=  2;     // Double  the
capacity
            int* newArr = new int[capacity];  //
Allocate new memory
            for (int i = 0; i < size; i++) {
                newArr[i]  =  arr[i];    //    old
elements to the new array
            }
            delete[] arr;  // Free the old memory
            arr = newArr;   // Point to the new
memory
        }
        arr[size] = element;  // Add new element
        size++;
    }

    void display() {
        for (int i = 0; i < size; i++) {
            cout << arr[i] << " ";
        }
        cout << endl;
    }

    ~DynamicArray() {
        delete[] arr;    // Free  the  allocated
memory when the object is destroyed
    }
};
```

```
int main() {
    DynamicArray arr;

    // Adding elements to the dynamic array
    arr.addElement(10);
    arr.addElement(20);
    arr.addElement(30);
    arr.addElement(40);

    // Displaying the array
    arr.display();

    return 0;
}
```

Explanation:

1. The `DynamicArray` class contains an array (`arr`) that is dynamically allocated. It has an initial capacity and starts with a size of 0.

2. The `addElement()` method adds elements to the array. If the array is full (i.e., `size == capacity`), it doubles the capacity, creates a new larger array, and copies the old elements to the new array.

3. The destructor `~DynamicArray()` frees the dynamically allocated memory when the object is destroyed.

In the example, when more elements are added, the array dynamically resizes, allowing the program to efficiently handle additional data.

Summary:

By the end of this chapter, you should be comfortable with:

- **Dynamic memory allocation** using `new` and `delete` and preventing memory leaks.
- **Pointers and references**, and how they are used for indirect data manipulation.
- **Memory management functions** like `new[]`, `delete[]`, `malloc`, and `free` in C++.
- A **real-world example** of building a **dynamic array** that resizes as elements are added, illustrating efficient memory management in C++.

In the next chapter, we will explore **advanced C++ topics** such as **multithreading**, **smart pointers**, and **file handling** to enhance your programming skills further.

CHAPTER 9

UNDERSTANDING C++ TEMPLATES

Introduction to Templates

In C++, **templates** allow you to write generic and reusable code. Templates enable the creation of functions, classes, or data structures that can operate on **any data type**, making your code more flexible and adaptable without sacrificing type safety.

Templates provide a way to write a single function or class definition that can work with multiple data types, allowing the compiler to generate the appropriate code at compile time based on the types used.

There are two primary types of templates in C++:

1. **Function Templates**: Used to create functions that can work with any data type.
2. **Class Templates**: Used to create classes that can work with any data type.

Templates are particularly useful for tasks like **creating containers, algorithms**, and **data structures** that need to work with various types without duplicating code for each type.

Function Templates

A **function template** defines a function that can work with **any data type**. The data type is specified by the programmer when the function is called.

Syntax of Function Templates:

To define a function template, use the `template` keyword followed by the type parameter inside angle brackets (<>).

cpp

```
template <typename T>
T add(T a, T b) {
    return a + b;
}
```

- **template <typename T>**: This declares a template, where T is a placeholder for any data type.
- The add() function can now be called with any type (like int, double, float, etc.).

Example: Function Template

cpp

```cpp
#include <iostream>
using namespace std;

template <typename T>
T multiply(T a, T b) {
    return a * b;   // Multiplies two values of
any type
}

int main() {
    cout << "Multiplication of integers: " <<
multiply(5, 3) << endl;
    cout << "Multiplication of doubles: " <<
multiply(3.5, 2.1) << endl;
    return 0;
}
```

Explanation:

- The `multiply()` function works for any data type, whether it's integers or floating-point numbers.
- When calling `multiply(5, 3)`, the template is instantiated with `T = int`. When calling `multiply(3.5, 2.1)`, the template is instantiated with `T = double`.

Class Templates

A **class template** defines a class that can operate on **any data type**. Like function templates, class templates allow for the creation of classes that work with different types, avoiding the need to write separate versions of the class for each type.

Syntax of Class Templates:

The `template` keyword is used before the class definition, with the type parameter inside angle brackets.

cpp

```cpp
template <typename T>
class Box {
private:
    T value;   // This will hold a value of any type T

public:
    Box(T val) : value(val) {}  // Constructor

    T getValue() {
        return value;
    }

    void setValue(T val) {
```

```
        value = val;
    }
};
```

- **Box(T val)**: The class constructor takes a parameter of type T.
- The getValue() and setValue() methods work with type T, making the Box class generic.

Example: Class Template

cpp

```cpp
#include <iostream>
using namespace std;

template <typename T>
class Box {
private:
    T value;

public:
    Box(T val) : value(val) {}

    T getValue() {
        return value;
    }

    void setValue(T val) {
        value = val;
```

```
    }
};

int main() {
    // Creating objects of Box class with
different types
    Box<int> intBox(10);   // Box for integers
    Box<double> doubleBox(5.5);    // Box for
doubles

    cout << "Integer box contains: " <<
intBox.getValue() << endl;
    cout << "Double box contains: " <<
doubleBox.getValue() << endl;

    intBox.setValue(20);    // Update value in
intBox
    doubleBox.setValue(10.1); // Update value in
doubleBox

    cout << "Updated integer box contains: " <<
intBox.getValue() << endl;
    cout << "Updated double box contains: " <<
doubleBox.getValue() << endl;

    return 0;
}
```

Explanation:

- The `Box` class template can hold any data type, such as integers and doubles, as demonstrated in the `main()` function.
- The class is instantiated with the `int` type and `double` type, showing how templates can be used to create reusable classes.

Real-World Example: A Generic Sorting Function That Works with Different Data Types

One of the most common uses of templates is to create generic algorithms like **sorting**. Let's create a template function that sorts an array of any data type using the **bubble sort** algorithm.

Sorting Function Template

cpp

```cpp
#include <iostream>
using namespace std;

template <typename T>
void bubbleSort(T arr[], int size) {
    for (int i = 0; i < size - 1; i++) {
        for (int j = 0; j < size - i - 1; j++) {
            if (arr[j] > arr[j + 1]) {
                // Swap elements
                T temp = arr[j];
```

```cpp
                arr[j] = arr[j + 1];
                arr[j + 1] = temp;
            }
        }
    }
}


template <typename T>
void printArray(T arr[], int size) {
    for (int i = 0; i < size; i++) {
        cout << arr[i] << " ";
    }
    cout << endl;
}


int main() {
    // Sorting an array of integers
    int intArr[] = {5, 2, 9, 1, 5, 6};
    int      size      =      sizeof(intArr)      /
sizeof(intArr[0]);

    cout << "Original integer array: ";
    printArray(intArr, size);
    bubbleSort(intArr, size);
    cout << "Sorted integer array: ";
    printArray(intArr, size);

    // Sorting an array of doubles
    double doubleArr[] = {2.3, 1.5, 4.7, 3.1};
```

```
    int     sizeD    =     sizeof(doubleArr)     /
sizeof(doubleArr[0]);

    cout << "Original double array: ";
    printArray(doubleArr, sizeD);
    bubbleSort(doubleArr, sizeD);
    cout << "Sorted double array: ";
    printArray(doubleArr, sizeD);

    return 0;
}
```

Explanation:

- **bubbleSort()**: This function template sorts an array of any data type (T), whether integers or doubles.
- The sorting algorithm works by comparing adjacent elements and swapping them if they are in the wrong order. This continues until the array is sorted.
- **printArray()**: This function template is used to print the elements of the array, and it works with any data type.

Why Use Templates for Sorting?

Templates allow you to reuse the bubbleSort() function for different data types, making the code more flexible and reducing redundancy. The same function works for sorting arrays of integers, doubles, or any other type, providing **type safety** and **flexibility**.

Summary:

By the end of this chapter, you should have a clear understanding of:

- **C++ Templates** and their role in writing generic, reusable code.
- **Function Templates**: How to create functions that can work with different data types.
- **Class Templates**: How to create classes that can handle multiple data types.
- **Real-World Example**: Implementing a **generic sorting function** that works with different data types.

In the next chapter, we will dive deeper into **advanced template features**, such as **template specialization** and **variadic templates**, to further enhance the flexibility and power of templates in C++.

CHAPTER 10

EXCEPTION HANDLING IN C++

Introduction to Errors and Exceptions

In every program, there is the possibility of encountering errors during runtime, which can disrupt the normal flow of execution. These errors can be caused by various factors, such as invalid user input, file access problems, or out-of-memory conditions.

C++ provides a mechanism called **exception handling** to deal with errors gracefully and maintain program stability. Exception handling allows you to catch errors and handle them in a way that doesn't cause the entire program to crash.

There are two main types of errors:

- **Syntax errors**: Errors in the program's code that prevent it from compiling (e.g., missing semicolons, incorrect syntax).
- **Runtime errors**: Errors that occur during the execution of the program, such as dividing by zero, accessing invalid memory, or opening a non-existent file.

Exception handling is specifically designed to handle **runtime errors**.

Try, Catch, Throw

C++ uses three keywords to handle exceptions: **try**, **catch**, and **throw**.

1. try Block:

The try block contains the code that might throw an exception. If an exception is thrown, the program immediately jumps to the corresponding catch block.

2. throw Statement:

The throw statement is used to signal that an exception has occurred. It is followed by an object representing the error or exception type.

3. catch Block:

The catch block catches exceptions thrown by the try block and allows the program to handle the exception in a controlled manner. You can have multiple catch blocks to handle different types of exceptions.

Basic Syntax:

cpp

```cpp
try {
    // Code that might throw an exception
} catch (exception_type1 e1) {
    // Handle exception of type exception_type1
} catch (exception_type2 e2) {
    // Handle exception of type exception_type2
} catch (...) {
    // Catch any exception
}
```

Example: Handling a Division by Zero Error

cpp

```cpp
#include <iostream>
using namespace std;

int divide(int a, int b) {
    if (b == 0) {
        throw "Division by zero error";  // Throw
an exception
    }
    return a / b;
}

int main() {
    int num1 = 10, num2 = 0;
```

```
    try {
        int result = divide(num1, num2);
        cout << "Result: " << result << endl;
    } catch (const char* msg) {
        cout << "Error: " << msg << endl;    //
Handle the exception
    }

    return 0;
}
```

Explanation:

- The `divide()` function throws an exception if the second parameter is zero.
- The `catch` block handles the exception and prints an error message.

Custom Exception Classes

C++ allows you to create **custom exception classes** to handle specific types of errors in a more structured manner. You can define a custom exception class by inheriting from the base `std::exception` class or any of its derived classes.

Creating a Custom Exception Class:

To create a custom exception, inherit from `std::exception` and override the `what()` method, which returns an error message as a string.

Example:

cpp

```cpp
#include <iostream>
#include <exception>
using namespace std;

class InvalidInputException : public exception {
public:
    const char* what() const noexcept override {
        return "Invalid input error occurred.";
    }
};

int main() {
    try {
        throw InvalidInputException();  // Throw
custom exception
    } catch (const InvalidInputException& e) {
        cout << e.what() << endl;  // Handle
custom exception
    }
```

```
    return 0;
}
```

Explanation:

- `InvalidInputException` is a custom exception class that inherits from `std::exception`.
- The `what()` method is overridden to return a custom error message when the exception is caught.

Custom exception classes help make your error handling more descriptive and organized, as they allow you to define specific exceptions for different error conditions.

Real-World Example: Creating an Error-Handling Mechanism in a File Reading Program

A common scenario where exception handling is useful is when working with **file input/output (I/O)**. Trying to open a file that doesn't exist or attempting to read from a file without proper permissions can lead to runtime errors.

Let's build a simple program that reads content from a file and handles any errors that may occur during the process using exception handling.

File Reading Program with Error Handling:

cpp

```cpp
#include <iostream>
#include <fstream>
#include <stdexcept>  // For std::runtime_error
using namespace std;

void readFile(const string& filename) {
    ifstream file(filename);

    if (!file) {
        throw runtime_error("Error: Unable to open the file.");
    }

    string line;
    while (getline(file, line)) {
        cout << line << endl;  // Print each line of the file
    }

    file.close();
}

int main() {
    string filename = "example.txt";

    try {
```

```
        readFile(filename);    // Attempt to read
the file
    } catch (const runtime_error& e) {
        cout << e.what() << endl;  // Handle file
opening error
    }

    return 0;
}
```

Explanation:

- The `readFile()` function attempts to open the file specified by `filename` using an `ifstream` object.
- If the file cannot be opened (e.g., it doesn't exist), a `runtime_error` exception is thrown with a relevant error message.
- The `catch` block in the `main()` function handles the exception and prints the error message.

Why Use Exception Handling Here?

- Using exception handling helps separate the error detection and handling logic from the main program logic, making the code more readable.
- Instead of manually checking for errors every time you perform a file operation (e.g., using `if` statements),

exception handling provides a clean and structured way to manage runtime errors.

Summary:

By the end of this chapter, you should be familiar with:

- **Exception handling** in C++ and how it provides a structured way to handle runtime errors using `try`, `catch`, and `throw`.
- How to create **custom exception classes** to handle specific types of errors.
- **Real-world examples** like handling file read errors, which demonstrate how exception handling can improve program robustness and readability.

In the next chapter, we will explore **multithreading** in C++, covering concepts such as creating and managing threads, synchronization, and avoiding race conditions.

CHAPTER 11

FILE I/O IN C++

Reading and Writing Files

File Input/Output (I/O) in C++ allows your programs to interact with files on the disk. Through file I/O operations, you can **read** data from files and **write** data to files. This is essential for programs that need to store or retrieve persistent data, such as configuration settings, logs, or game save files.

In C++, file I/O is handled using **file streams**. C++ provides different types of file streams to read from and write to files.

File Streams: `ifstream, ofstream`

C++ provides two primary classes for handling files:

1. **ifstream (Input File Stream)**: Used to read data from a file.

2. **ofstream (Output File Stream)**: Used to write data to a file.

3. **fstream**: A combination of `ifstream` and `ofstream`, used for both reading from and writing to a file.

127

Opening a File

To work with files, you must open them first. Files can be opened in different modes, such as:

- **ios::in**: Open the file for reading.
- **ios::out**: Open the file for writing.
- **ios::app**: Open the file in append mode, so data is added at the end.
- **ios::binary**: Open the file in binary mode, rather than text mode.

Example of Using ifstream and ofstream:

cpp

```cpp
#include <iostream>
#include <fstream>  // For file handling
#include <string>
using namespace std;

int main() {
    // Writing to a file using ofstream
    ofstream outputFile("example.txt");  // Open
the file for writing
    if (outputFile.is_open()) {
        outputFile << "Hello, C++ File I/O!" <<
endl;  // Write to the file
        outputFile << "This is an example of file
writing." << endl;
```

```
        outputFile.close();    // Close the file
after writing
    } else {
        cout << "Error opening the file for
writing!" << endl;
    }


    // Reading from the file using ifstream
    ifstream inputFile("example.txt");    // Open
the file for reading
    string line;
    if (inputFile.is_open()) {
        while (getline(inputFile, line)) {    //
Read line by line
            cout << line << endl;  // Output the
line
        }
        inputFile.close();    // Close the file
after reading
    } else {
        cout << "Error opening the file for
reading!" << endl;
    }

    return 0;
}
```

Explanation:

- The program first opens the file `example.txt` using `ofstream` for writing, writes a couple of lines of text, and then closes the file.
- Then it opens the same file using `ifstream`, reads it line by line, and prints the contents to the console.

Binary Files vs. Text Files

In C++, files can be opened in two different modes: **text mode** and **binary mode**.

Text Files:

Text files store data as human-readable text. When you open a file in text mode, data is stored as characters, with special handling for end-of-line characters (like \n in Unix/Linux and \r\n in Windows). This makes text files easy to read and edit manually.

- **Use cases**: Storing plain text, configuration files, logs, and serialized objects in a readable format.

Example: Writing and Reading Text Files

cpp

```cpp
ofstream textFile("textfile.txt");
```

```
textFile << "This is a line in a text file." <<
endl;
textFile.close();
```

Binary Files:

Binary files store data as raw bytes. This allows you to store more complex data (like objects or images) in their original format without any special character conversion. When you open a file in binary mode, no transformation is done on the data. It's ideal for saving non-text data, such as images, serialized objects, or game states.

- **Use cases**: Storing structured data (e.g., integers, floating-point numbers, custom objects) or non-text data (e.g., images, audio).

Example: Writing and Reading Binary Files

cpp

```cpp
#include <iostream>
#include <fstream>
using namespace std;

int main() {
    int number = 12345;

    // Writing to a binary file
```

```
    ofstream         binaryFile("binaryfile.dat",
ios::binary);

binaryFile.write(reinterpret_cast<char*>(&numbe
r), sizeof(number));
    binaryFile.close();

    // Reading from a binary file
    ifstream         readBinary("binaryfile.dat",
ios::binary);
    int readNumber;

readBinary.read(reinterpret_cast<char*>(&readNu
mber), sizeof(readNumber));
    readBinary.close();

    cout << "Read number: " << readNumber <<
endl;  // Outputs: 12345
    return 0;
}
```

Explanation:

- **Writing to a binary file**: The program writes the integer 12345 as raw binary data.
- **Reading from a binary file**: The program reads the raw binary data back into the integer variable readNumber.

- The **reinterpret_cast<char*>** is used to treat the address of the integer as a pointer to raw byte data, which is required for binary file operations.

Real-World Example: A Simple Program to Read from and Write to a Text File (e.g., a Text-Based Game's Save/Load Feature)

Let's now build a **simple text-based game** save/load feature using file I/O. In this example, we will store the player's name and score in a text file, and then allow the player to load the data from the file when the game restarts.

Game Save/Load Program:

cpp

```cpp
#include <iostream>
#include <fstream>
#include <string>
using namespace std;

class Player {
private:
    string name;
    int score;

public:
```

```cpp
    Player(string playerName = "Player", int
playerScore = 0)
        : name(playerName), score(playerScore)
{}

    void display() {
        cout << "Player: " << name << ", Score:
" << score << endl;
    }

    void saveToFile(const string& filename) {
        ofstream file(filename);
        if (file.is_open()) {
            file << name << endl;
            file << score << endl;
            file.close();
            cout << "Game saved!" << endl;
        } else {
            cout << "Error saving the game!" <<
endl;
        }
    }

    void loadFromFile(const string& filename) {
        ifstream file(filename);
        if (file.is_open()) {
            getline(file, name);  // Read player
name
```

```cpp
            file >> score;          // Read player
score
            file.close();
            cout << "Game loaded!" << endl;
        } else {
            cout << "Error loading the game!" <<
endl;
        }
    }
};

int main() {
    Player player1("Alice", 100);
    player1.display();

    // Save the player's game state to a file
    player1.saveToFile("game_save.txt");

    // Create a new player object and load the
saved game data
    Player player2;
    player2.loadFromFile("game_save.txt");
    player2.display();

    return 0;
}
```

Explanation:

- The Player class has two attributes: name and score.

- The `saveToFile()` method writes the player's name and score to a file called `"game_save.txt"`.
- The `loadFromFile()` method reads the player's data from the `"game_save.txt"` file, allowing the game to continue with the previously saved state.
- The **`getline()`** function is used to read the name (a string), and the `>>` operator is used to read the integer score from the file.
- If the file does not exist or cannot be opened, the program will print an error message.

Summary:

By the end of this chapter, you should:

- Understand how to read from and write to **text and binary files** in C++ using **`ifstream`** and **`ofstream`**.
- Be familiar with the differences between **text files** and **binary files**, and when to use each.
- Know how to implement a **real-world file handling example** such as a **save/load feature** for a game.

In the next chapter, we will dive into **advanced C++ topics** like **multithreading**, **smart pointers**, and **working with larger data structures** to handle complex application scenarios.

CHAPTER 12

WORKING WITH STRINGS IN C++

String Class Overview

In C++, strings are used to store and manipulate sequences of characters. There are two primary ways to work with strings:

1. **C-style strings**: A sequence of characters terminated by a null character (`'\0'`), commonly represented as an array of `chars`.

2. **std::string**: A more powerful, high-level string class provided by the C++ Standard Library. It allows for dynamic memory management and various useful string manipulation functions.

C++ String Class (`std::string`)

- **std::string** is a part of the C++ Standard Library, and it provides a rich set of features for working with strings.
- It automatically handles memory management, so you don't have to worry about the size or length of the string.
- Strings are mutable in `std::string`, meaning they can be modified after they are created.

137

Example of Using `std::string`:

cpp

```cpp
#include <iostream>
#include <string>
using namespace std;

int main() {
    string greeting = "Hello, C++!";
    cout << greeting << endl;
    return 0;
}
```

In this example, `greeting` is a string object that can store and manipulate a sequence of characters. The `std::string` class automatically manages memory for the string.

String Manipulations: Concatenation, Comparison, and Slicing

1. String Concatenation

Concatenation refers to combining two or more strings into one. This can be done using the + operator or the `append()` method.

- **Using the + operator:**

cpp

```cpp
string str1 = "Hello";
string str2 = "World";
string result = str1 + ", " + str2 + "!";
cout << result << endl;  // Outputs: Hello, World!
```

- **Using the append() method:**

cpp

```cpp
string str1 = "Hello";
str1.append(", World!");
cout << str1 << endl;  // Outputs: Hello, World!
```

2. String Comparison

You can compare strings using relational operators (==, !=, <, >, etc.). The comparison is done lexicographically, which means it compares the strings character by character based on ASCII values.

- **Comparing strings:**

cpp

```cpp
string str1 = "Hello";
string str2 = "World";

if (str1 == str2) {
    cout << "Strings are equal." << endl;
} else {
```

```cpp
    cout << "Strings are not equal." << endl;  // Outputs: Strings are not equal.
}
```

- **Using compare() method:**

cpp

```cpp
int result = str1.compare(str2);
if (result == 0) {
    cout << "Strings are equal." << endl;
} else if (result < 0) {
    cout << "str1 is less than str2." << endl;
} else {
    cout << "str1 is greater than str2." << endl;
}
```

3. String Slicing

You can extract a substring (slice) from a string using the substr() method. It allows you to specify the starting index and the length of the substring.

Example:

cpp

```cpp
string str = "Hello, World!";
string subStr = str.substr(7, 5);   // Extracts "World"
```

```
cout << subStr << endl;
```

- The `substr()` method extracts a portion of the string starting at index 7 and for a length of 5 characters.

4. String Length

You can find the length of a string using the `size()` or `length()` method, both of which return the number of characters in the string.

cpp

```
string str = "Hello";
cout << "Length of the string: " << str.size() << endl;   // Outputs: 5
```

Using `std::string` vs. C-style Strings

In C++, **C-style strings** are arrays of `char` terminated by a null character (`'\0'`). Although `std::string` is more modern and flexible, it's important to understand C-style strings because they are still widely used in legacy systems and low-level operations.

C-style Strings

- Declared as an array of characters.
- They are terminated by a `'\0'` character.

- Operations like concatenation and comparison require additional functions (`strcat()`, `strcmp()`, etc.) from the C standard library (`<cstring>`).

Example:

cpp

```cpp
#include <iostream>
#include <cstring>
using namespace std;

int main() {
    char str1[] = "Hello";
    char str2[] = "World";
    char result[50];

    strcpy(result, str1);  // str1 into result
    strcat(result, ", ");  // Concatenate ", " to
result
    strcat(result, str2);  // Concatenate str2 to
result

    cout << result << endl;  // Outputs: Hello,
World
    return 0;
}
```

- `strcpy()` copies one string into another.

- `strcat()` appends one string to another.

Limitations of C-style strings:

- You need to manually manage memory (e.g., ensuring the correct size of arrays).
- Functions like `strcat()` and `strcpy()` can cause **buffer overflows** if the destination string isn't large enough.

Advantages of `std::string`:

- **Automatic memory management**: `std::string` resizes dynamically, so you don't have to worry about buffer sizes.
- **Easier manipulation**: You can directly use operators like `+`, `==`, and methods like `substr()`, making `std::string` more convenient.
- **Type safety**: `std::string` avoids many of the common pitfalls of C-style strings (e.g., null terminators and manual memory management).

Real-World Example: A Program that Analyzes User Input (e.g., Parsing a Sentence for Keywords)

Let's build a real-world example where we create a program that asks the user to input a sentence, and then parses the sentence to search for specific keywords. This can be useful for applications like simple search engines, command parsers, or game dialogue systems.

Program Description:

1. The program asks the user for a sentence.
2. It looks for specific keywords in the sentence.
3. If the keyword is found, it prints a corresponding message.

Program Code:

cpp

```cpp
#include <iostream>
#include <sstream>   // For stringstream
#include <string>
using namespace std;

void findKeyword(const string& sentence, const string& keyword) {
    stringstream ss(sentence);
    string word;
```

```cpp
    bool found = false;

    while (ss >> word) {  // Read each word from
the sentence
        if (word == keyword) {
            cout << "Found the keyword: " <<
keyword << endl;
            found = true;
            break;
        }
    }

    if (!found) {
        cout << "Keyword not found: " << keyword
<< endl;
    }
}

int main() {
    string sentence;
    string keyword = "C++";

    cout << "Enter a sentence: ";
    getline(cin, sentence);  // Read the entire
line of input

    findKeyword(sentence, keyword);
```

145

```
    return 0;
}
```

Explanation:

- **stringstream**: This is used to split the input sentence into individual words. It helps in parsing and analyzing strings.
- The program uses a simple loop to check each word in the sentence against the keyword (C++ in this case).
- **getline()**: This function is used to read the entire line of input, which is important when the user's input contains spaces.

Summary:

By the end of this chapter, you should:

- Be comfortable working with **std::string**, using string manipulation techniques like concatenation, comparison, and slicing.
- Understand the difference between **std::string** and **C-style strings**, and know when to use each.
- Have learned how to handle **user input** and **parse strings** to search for keywords, which is useful in real-world applications like search engines or command-line tools.

In the next chapter, we will explore **advanced topics in C++**, including **multithreading**, **smart pointers**, and **working with complex data structures**.

CHAPTER 13

C++ CONCURRENCY AND MULTITHREADING

Introduction to Threads

In modern computing, **concurrency** refers to the ability of a system to handle multiple tasks simultaneously, making better use of the system's resources and improving performance. **Multithreading** is a form of concurrency where multiple threads (smaller units of a process) are executed in parallel. Each thread can execute its own part of a program, enabling more efficient processing, especially on multi-core processors.

- **Thread**: A thread is the smallest unit of execution in a program. It can run independently while sharing the same memory space with other threads in the same process.
- **Concurrency** allows multiple threads to make progress independently, but not necessarily at the same time.
- **Parallelism** occurs when threads are actually running simultaneously, typically on multi-core processors.

In C++, threads are supported by the **C++11 Standard** and above, which provides the <thread> library for managing threads.

Creating Threads in C++

To create threads in C++, you need to use the `<thread>` library, which provides the `std::thread` class. A thread is created by passing a function or callable object to the thread constructor.

Basic Syntax to Create a Thread:

cpp

```cpp
#include <iostream>
#include <thread>
using namespace std;

void printMessage() {
    cout << "Hello from thread!" << endl;
}

int main() {
    // Create and launch a thread
    thread t(printMessage);    // t is a thread
running the printMessage function

    // Wait for the thread to finish execution
    t.join();   // Join ensures the main thread
waits for t to complete before proceeding

    return 0;
}
```

Explanation:

- The std::thread constructor accepts a function name (printMessage), which it executes in a new thread.
- The join() method ensures that the main thread waits for the printMessage thread to finish before the program ends.

Passing Arguments to a Thread:

You can pass arguments to the function that the thread is running, just like regular functions.

cpp

```cpp
#include <iostream>
#include <thread>
using namespace std;

void printNumbers(int start, int end) {
    for (int i = start; i <= end; i++) {
        cout << i << " ";
    }
    cout << endl;
}

int main() {
    thread t1(printNumbers, 1, 5);   // Pass arguments to the thread
```

```
thread t2(printNumbers, 6, 10);

t1.join();
t2.join();

return 0;
}
```

In this example, two threads (t1 and t2) are created to print different ranges of numbers. The arguments 1, 5 and 6, 10 are passed to the printNumbers function.

Synchronization with Mutexes and Locks

When multiple threads access shared resources (such as data or memory), it can lead to **data races** and **undefined behavior**. To ensure that only one thread can access a shared resource at a time, **synchronization** is required. This is where **mutexes** and **locks** come in.

- **Mutex (Mutual Exclusion)**: A mutex is an object that prevents multiple threads from accessing a resource simultaneously. It acts as a lock, ensuring that only one thread can execute a critical section of code at a time.
- **Lock**: A lock is a mechanism to acquire a mutex, ensuring that a thread holds the mutex while working with the shared resource.

Using `std::mutex` for Synchronization:

cpp

```cpp
#include <iostream>
#include <thread>
#include <mutex>
using namespace std;

mutex mtx;   //. Mutex to protect shared resource

void printNumbers(int start, int end) {
    for (int i = start; i <= end; i++) {
        mtx.lock();   // Acquire the lock before accessing the shared resource
        cout << i << " ";
        mtx.unlock();   // Release the lock after accessing the resource
    }
    cout << endl;
}

int main() {
    thread t1(printNumbers, 1, 5);
    thread t2(printNumbers, 6, 10);

    t1.join();
    t2.join();

    return 0;
```

```
}
```

Explanation:

- The `mutex mtx` is used to synchronize access to the `cout` stream.
- `mtx.lock()` acquires the mutex, preventing other threads from accessing `cout` until the lock is released with `mtx.unlock()`.

Using `std::lock_guard` for Automatic Locking:

Instead of manually locking and unlocking a mutex, you can use **std::lock_guard**, which automatically locks the mutex when the `lock_guard` is created and unlocks it when the `lock_guard` goes out of scope.

cpp

```cpp
#include <iostream>
#include <thread>
#include <mutex>
using namespace std;

mutex mtx;

void printNumbers(int start, int end) {
    for (int i = start; i <= end; i++) {
```

```
        lock_guard<mutex>      lock(mtx);           //
Automatically locks the mutex
        cout << i << " ";
    }
    cout << endl;
}

int main() {
    thread t1(printNumbers, 1, 5);
    thread t2(printNumbers, 6, 10);

    t1.join();
    t2.join();

    return 0;
}
```

Explanation:

- The `lock_guard` automatically handles acquiring and releasing the lock, making the code simpler and safer by preventing common mistakes like forgetting to unlock the mutex.

Real-World Example: A Multi-threaded Downloader Application

In this example, we'll simulate a **multi-threaded downloader** that downloads different parts of a file concurrently. Each thread will simulate downloading a section of the file, and synchronization will be used to manage shared resources.

Downloader Program:

cpp

```cpp
#include <iostream>
#include <thread>
#include <mutex>
#include <chrono>   // For simulating download
time
using namespace std;

mutex mtx;   // Mutex to protect shared resources

void downloadPart(int part) {
    mtx.lock();
    cout << "Downloading part " << part << "..."
<< endl;
    mtx.unlock();

    // Simulating time taken to download a part
    this_thread::sleep_for(chrono::seconds(2));

    mtx.lock();
    cout << "Finished downloading part " << part
<< "." << endl;
    mtx.unlock();
}
```

```
int main() {
    // Creating multiple threads to download
different parts
    thread t1(downloadPart, 1);
    thread t2(downloadPart, 2);
    thread t3(downloadPart, 3);

    // Wait for all threads to finish
    t1.join();
    t2.join();
    t3.join();

    cout << "Download complete!" << endl;

    return 0;
}
```

Explanation:

- Each thread simulates downloading a part of a file. The download process is simulated using `sleep_for()` to delay the thread for 2 seconds, simulating the time taken for downloading a file part.
- The mutex `mtx` ensures that the output to the console is properly synchronized, preventing multiple threads from printing messages simultaneously and causing garbled output.

- The `join()` method ensures that the main thread waits for all download threads to complete before printing "Download complete!".

Summary:

By the end of this chapter, you should:

- Understand the basics of **multithreading** in C++ and how to create threads using the `std::thread` class.
- Learn how to **synchronize threads** using mutexes and locks to protect shared resources and avoid data races.
- Be familiar with **real-world applications** of multithreading, such as a **multi-threaded downloader** that improves performance by downloading multiple parts of a file simultaneously.

In the next chapter, we will explore **advanced C++ features** such as **smart pointers**, **RAII (Resource Acquisition Is Initialization)**, and **working with complex data structures**.

CHAPTER 14

INTRODUCTION TO C++11/14/17/20 FEATURES

Overview of Modern C++ Standards

C++ has evolved significantly over the years. The introduction of new standards (C++11, C++14, C++17, and C++20) has brought powerful features that improve the language's usability, efficiency, and safety. These standards introduced new tools for developers to write cleaner, faster, and more maintainable code.

Here's a quick look at the key C++ standards:

- **C++11**: Introduced many features like lambda expressions, the `auto` keyword, smart pointers, `nullptr`, and more. This version marked a significant evolution in C++.
- **C++14**: Mostly a bug-fixing release, but it improved existing features and added some new ones, like generic lambdas.
- **C++17**: Introduced features like structured bindings, `std::optional`, and parallel algorithms.

- **C++20**: This is the most recent standard, introducing concepts, ranges, coroutines, and more, further improving the expressiveness and safety of C++.

This chapter will cover some of the most important features introduced in **C++11**, **C++14**, **C++17**, and **C++20** that are commonly used in modern C++ programming.

Key Features in C++11 and Beyond

1. Lambdas (C++11)

Lambdas provide a concise way to define anonymous functions or function objects inline. They are especially useful for passing functions as arguments to algorithms like `std::for_each` or `std::sort`.

Syntax:

cpp

```
[ capture_clause ] ( parameter_list ) ->
return_type { function_body }
```

- **Capture clause** allows the lambda to capture variables from the surrounding scope.
- **Parameter list** is optional, just like regular function arguments.

- **Return type** is optional; it can be deduced from the return statement.

Example:

cpp

```cpp
#include <iostream>
#include <vector>
#include <algorithm>
using namespace std;

int main() {
    vector<int> nums = {1, 2, 3, 4, 5};

    // Lambda that prints each element
    for_each(nums.begin(), nums.end(), [](int x)
{
        cout << x << " ";
    });
    cout << endl;

    return 0;
}
```

Explanation:

- The lambda expression `[](int x) { cout << x <<` `" "; }` is passed to `for_each()` to print each element in the vector.

2. The `auto` Keyword (C++11)

The `auto` keyword allows for type inference, meaning that the compiler automatically deduces the type of a variable based on the initializer expression. This can reduce redundancy and make the code easier to maintain.

Example:

cpp

```
#include <iostream>
#include <vector>
using namespace std;

int main() {
    vector<int> nums = {1, 2, 3, 4, 5};

    // Using auto to automatically deduce the
iterator type
    for (auto it = nums.begin(); it !=
nums.end(); ++it) {
        cout << *it << " ";
    }
    cout << endl;
```

```
    return 0;
}
```

Explanation:

- The `auto` keyword is used to deduce the type of `it` (the iterator type of the vector), simplifying the code.

3. `nullptr` (C++11)

`nullptr` is a new keyword that represents a **null pointer**. It is type-safe, unlike the previous `NULL` macro, which could lead to issues in certain cases, especially with function overloading.

Example:

cpp

```cpp
#include <iostream>
using namespace std;

void foo(int* ptr) {
    if (ptr == nullptr) {
        cout << "Pointer is null" << endl;
    } else {
        cout << "Pointer is not null" << endl;
    }
}
```

```
int main() {
    int* ptr = nullptr;
    foo(ptr);  // Outputs: Pointer is null
    return 0;
}
```

Explanation:

- `nullptr` replaces `NULL` to check for null pointers in a more reliable way.

4. Smart Pointers (C++11)

Smart pointers are objects that manage dynamically allocated memory automatically. They help in preventing memory leaks and dangling pointers. The C++ Standard Library provides three types of smart pointers:

- **std::unique_ptr**: A smart pointer that owns a resource exclusively. It cannot be copied but can be moved.
- **std::shared_ptr**: A smart pointer that allows multiple pointers to share ownership of a resource.
- **std::weak_ptr**: A smart pointer that does not affect the reference count of a resource. It is used in situations where you don't want to extend the lifetime of the resource.

Example with `std::unique_ptr`:

cpp

```cpp
#include <iostream>
#include <memory>
using namespace std;

int main() {
    unique_ptr<int> p1 = make_unique<int>(10);
// Creates a unique pointer

    cout << "Value: " << *p1 << endl;   // Access
the value through dereferencing
    // p1 is automatically destroyed when it goes
out of scope
    return 0;
}
```

Explanation:

- `std::unique_ptr` automatically frees the memory it points to when it goes out of scope, preventing memory leaks.

Real-World Example: Refactoring an Older Program with Modern C++ Features

Let's consider an older C++ program that performs a simple task, such as calculating the sum of even numbers from 1 to 100. The program can be refactored to use modern C++ features such as **lambdas, `auto`**, and **`nullptr`**.

Old C++ Code (Pre-C++11):

cpp

```cpp
#include <iostream>
using namespace std;

int main() {
    int sum = 0;
    for (int i = 1; i <= 100; i++) {
        if (i % 2 == 0) {
            sum += i;
        }
    }
    cout << "Sum of even numbers: " << sum << endl;
    return 0;
}
```

Refactored C++ Code (Using C++11 and Beyond):

cpp

```cpp
#include <iostream>
#include <algorithm>
#include <vector>
using namespace std;

int main() {
    vector<int> nums(100);
    iota(nums.begin(), nums.end(), 1);   // Fill
the vector with numbers from 1 to 100

    // Use a lambda to calculate the sum of even
numbers
    int sum = 0;
    for_each(nums.begin(),            nums.end(),
[&sum](int num) {
        if (num % 2 == 0) {
            sum += num;
        }
    });

    cout << "Sum of even numbers: " << sum <<
endl;
    return 0;
}
```

Explanation of Refactored Code:

1. **iota()**: This function from the `<numeric>` library fills a range with sequential values. It's used here to populate the vector `nums` with values from 1 to 100.

2. **Lambda Expression**: The `for_each()` function is used along with a lambda expression to iterate over the vector and sum the even numbers. The `sum` variable is captured by reference using `[&sum]` to modify it inside the lambda.

3. **auto**: Used in the `for_each()` loop to avoid explicitly specifying the iterator type.

This refactored program is more concise, modern, and leverages the powerful features introduced in **C++11** and beyond, making it more readable and maintainable.

Summary:

By the end of this chapter, you should have a solid understanding of:

*   The evolution of **C++11, C++14, C++17**, and **C++20** and the key features introduced in these versions.
*   How to use **lambdas** for inline functions, **auto** for type inference, **nullptr** for null pointer safety, and **smart pointers** for automatic memory management.

- How to **refactor older C++ code** to take advantage of modern C++ features, making the code more efficient, safe, and maintainable.

In the next chapter, we will explore **advanced C++ techniques** such as **metaprogramming, template specialization**, and **type traits**, which will take your understanding of C++ to the next level.

CHAPTER 15

BUILDING GRAPHICAL USER INTERFACES (GUIS) IN C++

Introduction to GUI Development

Graphical User Interfaces (GUIs) provide a user-friendly way for users to interact with software applications through visual elements like windows, buttons, and text fields. Developing a GUI in C++ can significantly enhance user experience, as it offers a more interactive and intuitive interface than command-line programs.

C++ itself does not include any built-in GUI libraries, but there are several third-party libraries that provide the necessary tools for GUI development. Some of the most popular ones are:

- **Qt**: A powerful, cross-platform library for GUI development, widely used in both commercial and open-source applications. Qt is feature-rich, supports modern C++ features, and works across platforms (Windows, Linux, macOS).

- **SFML (Simple and Fast Multimedia Library)**: A multimedia library that includes basic GUI components along with support for graphics, sound, and network functionality. It is more lightweight than Qt and suitable for games or multimedia applications.

- **GTKmm**: A C++ wrapper for the GTK library, commonly used for Linux-based GUI applications.
- **wxWidgets**: A cross-platform GUI library for C++ that provides native-looking GUIs on Windows, macOS, and Linux.

In this chapter, we will focus on **Qt** for GUI development, as it is one of the most popular and versatile libraries in C++.

Using Libraries like Qt or SFML

Qt Overview:

Qt is a free and open-source widget toolkit for creating graphical user interfaces. It is widely used for building cross-platform applications with a native look and feel.

1. **Qt Widgets**: Provides standard GUI components such as buttons, text boxes, and labels.
2. **Qt Quick**: A declarative framework for building dynamic and touch-enabled user interfaces.
3. **Signal and Slot Mechanism**: Qt uses a powerful event-driven architecture with signals and slots, where signals

are emitted by objects (like buttons) and slots are functions that respond to those signals.

Setting Up Qt for C++ Development:

1. Install **Qt Creator**, the official IDE for Qt development, from the Qt website.
2. After installation, you can create Qt Widgets-based applications or use Qt Quick for more modern, fluid UIs.
3. Qt supports both **Visual Studio** and **Qt Creator** as IDEs for writing, debugging, and running applications.

Event Handling and GUI Widgets

In a GUI application, **event handling** is crucial because it allows the program to respond to user actions, such as clicks, key presses, or window resizing. Qt uses the **signals and slots mechanism** to handle events.

- **Signal**: A signal is emitted when an event occurs (e.g., a button is clicked).
- **Slot**: A slot is a function that reacts to the signal. It can be automatically connected to a signal, and when the signal is emitted, the corresponding slot is executed.

Basic Qt Widgets:

Qt provides a variety of standard widgets to create GUIs, such as:

- **QPushButton**: A button widget.
- **QLabel**: A widget for displaying text or images.
- **QLineEdit**: A widget for single-line text input.
- **QTextEdit**: A widget for multi-line text input.
- **QComboBox**: A drop-down list.
- **QListView**: A list of items, useful for creating lists or file explorers.

Example: Simple Event Handling in Qt:

cpp

```cpp
#include <QApplication>
#include <QPushButton>
#include <QMessageBox>

int main(int argc, char *argv[]) {
    QApplication app(argc, argv);  // Initialize
the application

    QPushButton button("Click Me!");
    QObject::connect(&button,
&QPushButton::clicked, [](){
        QMessageBox::information(nullptr,
"Message", "Button was clicked!");
    });
```

```
button.show();  // Show the button

return app.exec();  // Start the event loop
}
```

Explanation:

- **QPushButton** creates a button labeled "Click Me!".
- **QObject::connect()** connects the button's `clicked` signal to a lambda function that displays a message box when the button is clicked.
- **app.exec()** starts the event loop that handles user interactions.

Real-World Example: Creating a Simple To-Do List with a GUI Using Qt

Now that you have a basic understanding of how to work with Qt, let's build a simple **to-do list application**. This application will allow users to add, remove, and display tasks.

Steps to Build a To-Do List Application:

1. **Create a window** with a QLineEdit to input tasks.
2. **Use a QListWidget** to display tasks in the list.
3. **Use QPushButton** to add and remove tasks.

173

4. **Connect the buttons to actions** using signals and slots.

Complete Program Code:

cpp

```cpp
#include <QApplication>
#include <QWidget>
#include <QPushButton>
#include <QLineEdit>
#include <QListWidget>
#include <QVBoxLayout>
#include <QMessageBox>

class TodoApp : public QWidget {
    Q_OBJECT   // For Qt's signals and slots
mechanism

public:
    TodoApp() {
        // Create the layout
        QVBoxLayout*    layout    =    new
QVBoxLayout(this);

        // Create a QLineEdit for entering tasks
        taskInput = new QLineEdit(this);
        taskInput->setPlaceholderText("Enter
task here...");
        layout->addWidget(taskInput);
```

```cpp
        // Create a QListWidget to display tasks
        taskList = new QListWidget(this);
        layout->addWidget(taskList);

        // Create a QPushButton to add tasks
        addButton = new QPushButton("Add Task",
this);
        layout->addWidget(addButton);

        // Create a QPushButton to remove
selected tasks
        removeButton = new QPushButton("Remove
Task", this);
        layout->addWidget(removeButton);

        // Connect signals to slots
        connect(addButton,
&QPushButton::clicked, this, &TodoApp::addTask);
        connect(removeButton,
&QPushButton::clicked,                       this,
&TodoApp::removeTask);

        // Set the layout for the main window
        setLayout(layout);
        setWindowTitle("To-Do List");
        resize(300, 400);
    }

private slots:
```

```cpp
void addTask() {
    QString task = taskInput->text();
    if (!task.isEmpty()) {
        taskList->addItem(task);
        taskInput->clear();
    } else {
        QMessageBox::warning(this,      "Input
Error", "Please enter a task.");
    }
}


void removeTask() {
    QListWidgetItem*      selectedItem      =
taskList->currentItem();
    if (selectedItem) {
        delete selectedItem;
    } else {
        QMessageBox::warning(this,
"Selection  Error",  "Please  select  a  task  to
remove.");
    }
}

private:
    QLineEdit* taskInput;
    QListWidget* taskList;
    QPushButton* addButton;
    QPushButton* removeButton;
};
```

```
int main(int argc, char *argv[]) {
    QApplication app(argc, argv);

    TodoApp window;
    window.show();

    return app.exec();
}
```

```
#include "main.moc"
```

Explanation:

- The program uses **QLineEdit** for task input, **QListWidget** for displaying tasks, and **QPushButton** for adding and removing tasks.
- **addTask()**: Adds a task to the list if it is not empty.
- **removeTask()**: Removes the selected task from the list. If no task is selected, it shows a warning message.
- **Signals and Slots**: The buttons are connected to the addTask() and removeTask() slots using Qt's signal-slot mechanism.

Key Features of the To-Do List Application:

- **QLineEdit**: Used for entering text. It allows users to type in a task.
- **QListWidget**: Displays a list of tasks. Users can click on tasks to select them.
- **QPushButton**: Buttons used for adding and removing tasks.
- **Signals and Slots**: Qt's event-handling system connects button clicks (signals) to appropriate actions (slots), such as adding or removing tasks.

Summary:

By the end of this chapter, you should:

- Understand how to **create and design GUIs in C++** using the **Qt** library.
- Be familiar with key Qt widgets like **QPushButton, QLineEdit**, and **QListWidget**.
- Have learned how to handle **events** and **user interactions** in a GUI through Qt's **signals and slots** mechanism.
- Have created a **real-world example**: A simple to-do list application with Qt.

In the next chapter, we will explore **advanced GUI techniques**, including **custom widgets**, **animations**, and **multithreading in GUIs**, to enhance your C++ GUI development skills.

CHAPTER 16

WORKING WITH DATA STRUCTURES

Introduction to Common Data Structures

Data structures are fundamental to computer science and programming. They are used to organize, store, and manipulate data efficiently. Choosing the right data structure is crucial for improving the performance of algorithms, especially in tasks that require searching, sorting, or managing large datasets.

Common data structures can be categorized into two main types:

- **Linear Data Structures**: Elements are arranged sequentially, where each element is connected to the next. Examples include **arrays**, **linked lists**, **stacks**, and **queues**.
- **Non-Linear Data Structures**: Elements are not arranged sequentially. Examples include **trees** and **graphs**, which are used for hierarchical and interconnected data.

In this chapter, we will explore some of these commonly used data structures and their applications in real-world scenarios.

Arrays, Linked Lists, Stacks, and Queues

1. Arrays

An **array** is a collection of elements of the same data type, stored in contiguous memory locations. Arrays are simple and efficient for indexing, but their size is fixed at the time of creation.

- **Key Features**:
    - **Indexing**: You can access elements by their index.
    - **Fixed Size**: The size of the array is defined when it is created and cannot be changed.

Example:

cpp

```
#include <iostream>
using namespace std;

int main() {
    int arr[5] = {1, 2, 3, 4, 5};

    // Access elements
    cout << "First element: " << arr[0] << endl;
// Outputs: 1
    return 0;
```

```
}
```

2. Linked Lists

A **linked list** is a linear data structure where elements (called nodes) are stored in memory as individual objects, and each node points to the next node in the sequence. This allows for dynamic sizing, unlike arrays.

- **Key Features**:
    o **Dynamic Size**: You can add or remove elements dynamically.
    o **Non-contiguous Memory**: Each node is stored separately in memory.

Example:

cpp

```cpp
#include <iostream>
using namespace std;

struct Node {
    int data;
    Node* next;
};

int main() {
    Node* head = new Node;
    head->data = 10;
```

```
    head->next = nullptr;

    cout << "First node data: " << head->data <<
endl;   // Outputs: 10
    delete head;   // Free the allocated memory
    return 0;
}
```

3. Stacks

A **stack** is a collection of elements that follows the **LIFO (Last In, First Out)** principle. The last element added to the stack is the first one to be removed.

- **Key Operations**:
  - **push()**: Adds an element to the top of the stack.
  - **pop()**: Removes the top element from the stack.
  - **peek()**: Returns the top element without removing it.

Example:

cpp

```cpp
#include <iostream>
#include <stack>
using namespace std;

int main() {
    stack<int> s;
```

```
    s.push(10);
    s.push(20);
    s.push(30);

    cout << "Top element: " << s.top() << endl;
// Outputs: 30
    s.pop();
    cout << "Top element after pop: " << s.top()
<< endl;   // Outputs: 20
    return 0;
}
```

4. Queues

A **queue** is a collection of elements that follows the **FIFO (First In, First Out)** principle. The first element added to the queue is the first one to be removed.

- **Key Operations**:
    o **enqueue()**: Adds an element to the back of the queue.
    o **dequeue()**: Removes the front element from the queue.
    o **front()**: Returns the front element without removing it.

Example:

cpp

184

```
#include <iostream>
#include <queue>
using namespace std;

int main() {
    queue<int> q;
    q.push(10);
    q.push(20);
    q.push(30);

    cout << "Front element: " << q.front() <<
endl;  // Outputs: 10
    q.pop();
    cout << "Front element after pop: " <<
q.front() << endl;  // Outputs: 20
    return 0;
}
```

Trees and Graphs

1. Trees

A **tree** is a hierarchical data structure that consists of nodes connected by edges. Each tree has one **root** node and zero or more child nodes. Trees are used in scenarios where hierarchical relationships are needed, such as file systems, XML data, and binary search trees.

- **Types of Trees**:

185

o **Binary Tree**: Each node has at most two children.

o **Binary Search Tree (BST)**: A binary tree where the left child is smaller than the parent node, and the right child is larger.

Example of a Binary Tree:

cpp

```cpp
#include <iostream>
using namespace std;

struct Node {
    int data;
    Node* left;
    Node* right;

    Node(int val) : data(val), left(nullptr),
right(nullptr) {}
};

void inorderTraversal(Node* root) {
    if (root != nullptr) {
        inorderTraversal(root->left);
        cout << root->data << " ";
        inorderTraversal(root->right);
    }
}
```

```
int main() {
    Node* root = new Node(10);
    root->left = new Node(5);
    root->right = new Node(15);
    .

    cout << "Inorder Traversal: ";
    inorderTraversal(root);   // Outputs: 5 10 15
    return 0;
}
```

Explanation:

- The binary tree is created with the root node having a value of 10. The left child is 5, and the right child is 15. The `inorderTraversal` function prints the values in the order 5, 10, 15.

2. Graphs

A **graph** is a collection of nodes (vertices) and edges that connect pairs of nodes. Graphs can be **directed** or **undirected**, and they are used to model relationships such as social networks, road networks, and dependency graphs.

- **Types of Graphs**:
    - **Directed Graph (Digraph)**: Edges have a direction (e.g., one-way street).

o **Undirected Graph**: Edges have no direction (e.g., two-way street).

o **Weighted Graph**: Edges have weights (e.g., distances between cities).

Example of an Undirected Graph (using adjacency list):

cpp

```cpp
#include <iostream>
#include <vector>
using namespace std;

class Graph {
public:
    vector<vector<int>> adjList;   // Adjacency
list to store graph

    Graph(int vertices) {
        adjList.resize(vertices);
    }

    void addEdge(int u, int v) {
        adjList[u].push_back(v);
        adjList[v].push_back(u);   // Undirected
graph
    }

    void display() {
```

```cpp
        for (int i = 0; i < adjList.size(); i++)
{

        cout << i << ": ";
        for (int j : adjList[i]) {
            cout << j << " ";
        }
        cout << endl;

    }

};

int main() {
    Graph g(5);  // Create a graph with 5 vertices

    g.addEdge(0, 1);
    g.addEdge(0, 2);
    g.addEdge(1, 3);
    g.addEdge(3, 4);

    cout << "Graph adjacency list: " << endl;
    g.display();
    return 0;
}
```

Explanation:

- The graph is represented using an adjacency list, where each index of the vector holds a list of nodes connected to it.

- The `addEdge` method adds an undirected edge between nodes u and v.

Real-World Example: A Search and Retrieval System Using Trees and Graphs

Let's combine **trees** and **graphs** to build a **search and retrieval system**. In this example, we will create a simple **directory structure** (tree) and use a **graph** to represent relationships between documents in a search index.

Example Code:

cpp

```cpp
#include <iostream>
#include <unordered_map>
#include <vector>
#include <string>
using namespace std;

class DirectoryTree {
private:
    unordered_map<string, vector<string>> tree;

public:
    void addDirectory(const string& parent,
const string& child) {
```

```cpp
            tree[parent].push_back(child);
    }


    void displayDirectories(const string& dir) {
        cout << dir << " contains: ";
        for (const auto& child : tree[dir]) {
            cout << child << " ";
        }
        cout << endl;
    }
};


class DocumentGraph {
private:
    unordered_map<string,         vector<string>>
docGraph;


public:
    void addDocumentRelation(const string& doc1,
const string& doc2) {
        docGraph[doc1].push_back(doc2);
    }


    void displayRelatedDocs(const string& doc) {
        cout << doc << " is related to: ";
        for    (const    auto&    relatedDoc    :
docGraph[doc]) {
            cout << relatedDoc << " ";
        }
```

```
        cout << endl;
    }
};

int main() {
    DirectoryTree dirTree;
    dirTree.addDirectory("root", "Documents");
    dirTree.addDirectory("Documents", "Work");
    dirTree.addDirectory("Documents",
"Personal");

    dirTree.displayDirectories("Documents");

    DocumentGraph docGraph;
    docGraph.addDocumentRelation("Document1",
"Document2");
    docGraph.addDocumentRelation("Document1",
"Document3");

    docGraph.displayRelatedDocs("Document1");

    return 0;
}
```

Explanation:

- **DirectoryTree**: Represents a directory structure using a tree. It allows you to add directories and display their contents.

- **DocumentGraph**: Represents document relationships (e.g., references, dependencies) using a graph.
- The program shows how data can be organized using trees (directories) and graphs (document relationships) to build a search and retrieval system.

Summary:

By the end of this chapter, you should have a solid understanding of:

- **Linear Data Structures**: Arrays, linked lists, stacks, and queues.
- **Non-linear Data Structures**: Trees and graphs, and how they are used in various applications.
- How to implement **basic trees and graphs** in C++ and apply them to real-world problems like search and retrieval systems.

In the next chapter, we will explore **advanced algorithms** used in conjunction with these data structures, such as searching, sorting, and graph traversal techniques.

CHAPTER 17

SORTING AND SEARCHING ALGORITHMS

Introduction to Sorting Algorithms

Sorting algorithms are used to arrange elements in a particular order, typically in ascending or descending order. Sorting is one of the most fundamental operations in computer science because it forms the basis for many other algorithms, including search algorithms. In this section, we will discuss three common sorting algorithms:

- **Bubble Sort**
- **Merge Sort**
- **QuickSort**

1. Bubble Sort

Bubble Sort is one of the simplest sorting algorithms, but it is also one of the least efficient for large datasets. It works by repeatedly swapping adjacent elements if they are in the wrong order, "bubbling" the largest unsorted element to the end of the array.

Time Complexity:

- Best case: O(n) (when the array is already sorted)
- Average case: $O(n^2)$
- Worst case: $O(n^2)$

Example:

cpp

```cpp
#include <iostream>
using namespace std;

void bubbleSort(int arr[], int n) {
    for (int i = 0; i < n-1; i++) {
        for (int j = 0; j < n-i-1; j++) {
            if (arr[j] > arr[j+1]) {
                swap(arr[j], arr[j+1]);
            }
        }
    }
}

int main() {
    int arr[] = {64, 34, 25, 12, 22, 11, 90};
    int n = sizeof(arr) / sizeof(arr[0]);

    bubbleSort(arr, n);

    cout << "Sorted array: ";
    for (int i = 0; i < n; i++) {
```

```
        cout << arr[i] << " ";
    }
    cout << endl;

    return 0;
}
```

Explanation:

- The `bubbleSort()` function performs multiple passes through the array, swapping adjacent elements to sort them.
- It uses two loops: one to control the number of passes and another to compare adjacent elements.

2. Merge Sort

Merge Sort is a **divide-and-conquer** algorithm. It splits the array into two halves, recursively sorts each half, and then merges the sorted halves to produce a fully sorted array.

Time Complexity:

- Best, Average, and Worst case: O(n log n)

Example:

cpp

```cpp
#include <iostream>
using namespace std;

void merge(int arr[], int l, int m, int r) {
    int n1 = m - l + 1;
    int n2 = r - m;

    int L[n1], R[n2];

    for (int i = 0; i < n1; i++) L[i] = arr[l + i];
    for (int i = 0; i < n2; i++) R[i] = arr[m + 1 + i];

    int i = 0, j = 0, k = l;
    while (i < n1 && j < n2) {
        if (L[i] <= R[j]) {
            arr[k++] = L[i++];
        } else {
            arr[k++] = R[j++];
        }
    }

    while (i < n1) arr[k++] = L[i++];
    while (j < n2) arr[k++] = R[j++];
}

void mergeSort(int arr[], int l, int r) {
    if (l < r) {
```

```
        int m = l + (r - l) / 2;
        mergeSort(arr, l, m);
        mergeSort(arr, m + 1, r);
        merge(arr, l, m, r);
    }
}

int main() {
    int arr[] = {12, 11, 13, 5, 6, 7};
    int n = sizeof(arr) / sizeof(arr[0]);

    mergeSort(arr, 0, n - 1);

    cout << "Sorted array: ";
    for (int i = 0; i < n; i++) {
        cout << arr[i] << " ";
    }
    cout << endl;

    return 0;
}
```

Explanation:

- The mergeSort() function recursively divides the array into two halves until the base case is reached (array of one element).
- The merge() function then combines two sorted halves into one sorted array.

198

3. QuickSort

QuickSort is another **divide-and-conquer** sorting algorithm. It picks a **pivot** element from the array and partitions the other elements into two sub-arrays (elements smaller than the pivot and elements greater than the pivot). The sub-arrays are recursively sorted.

Time Complexity:

- Best and Average case: $O(n \log n)$
- Worst case: $O(n^2)$ (can be avoided with good pivot selection strategies)

Example:

cpp

```cpp
#include <iostream>
using namespace std;

int partition(int arr[], int low, int high) {
    int pivot = arr[high];
    int i = (low - 1);
    for (int j = low; j <= high - 1; j++) {
        if (arr[j] <= pivot) {
            i++;
            swap(arr[i], arr[j]);
        }
```

199

```
    }
    swap(arr[i + 1], arr[high]);
    return (i + 1);
}


void quickSort(int arr[], int low, int high) {
    if (low < high) {
        int pi = partition(arr, low, high);

        quickSort(arr, low, pi - 1);
        quickSort(arr, pi + 1, high);
    }
}


int main() {
    int arr[] = {10, 7, 8, 9, 1, 5};
    int n = sizeof(arr) / sizeof(arr[0]);

    quickSort(arr, 0, n - 1);

    cout << "Sorted array: ";
    for (int i = 0; i < n; i++) {
        cout << arr[i] << " ";
    }
    cout << endl;

    return 0;
}
```

Explanation:

- `partition()` function rearranges the elements so that all elements less than the pivot are on the left, and those greater are on the right.
- `quickSort()` recursively applies this partitioning on sub-arrays until the entire array is sorted.

Searching Algorithms

Searching algorithms are used to find an element in a collection (e.g., an array or list). The two most commonly used searching algorithms are **Linear Search** and **Binary Search**.

1. Linear Search

Linear Search is the simplest searching algorithm. It checks each element in the array one by one to find the target value.

Time Complexity:

- Best case: O(1) (if the target is the first element)
- Worst case: O(n) (if the target is not in the array)

Example:

cpp

```
#include <iostream>
using namespace std;
```

```cpp
int linearSearch(int arr[], int size, int target)
{
    for (int i = 0; i < size; i++) {
        if (arr[i] == target) {
            return i;   // Return index if target
is found
        }
    }
    return -1;   // Return -1 if target is not
found
}

int main() {
    int arr[] = {5, 2, 9, 1, 5, 6};
    int target = 9;
    int size = sizeof(arr) / sizeof(arr[0]);

    int result = linearSearch(arr, size, target);
    if (result != -1) {
        cout << "Element found at index: " <<
result << endl;
    } else {
        cout << "Element not found!" << endl;
    }

    return 0;
}
```

2. Binary Search

Binary Search is a more efficient algorithm, but it only works on **sorted arrays**. It repeatedly divides the search interval in half, checking the middle element. If the target is smaller than the middle element, the search continues on the left half; otherwise, it continues on the right half.

Time Complexity:

- Best, Average, and Worst case: O(log n)

Example:

cpp

```cpp
#include <iostream>
using namespace std;

int binarySearch(int arr[], int size, int target)
{
    int left = 0, right = size - 1;
    while (left <= right) {
        int mid = left + (right - left) / 2;
        if (arr[mid] == target) {
            return mid;    // Return index if target is found
        }
        if (arr[mid] < target) {
```

```cpp
            left = mid + 1;    // Search in the
right half
        } else {
            right = mid - 1;   // Search in the
left half
        }
    }
    return -1;   // Return -1 if target is not
found
}

int main() {
    int arr[] = {1, 2, 3, 4, 5, 6, 7, 8, 9};
    int target = 6;
    int size = sizeof(arr) / sizeof(arr[0]);

    int result = binarySearch(arr, size, target);
    if (result != -1) {
        cout << "Element found at index: " <<
result << endl;
    } else {
        cout << "Element not found!" << endl;
    }

    return 0;
}
```

Real-World Example: Implementing an Address Book with Search and Sort Features

Now, let's combine **sorting** and **searching** algorithms to implement a simple **address book** that allows users to add, sort, and search for contacts.

Address Book Program Code:

cpp

```cpp
#include <iostream>
#include <vector>
#include <algorithm>  // For sort
using namespace std;

struct Contact {
    string name;
    string phoneNumber;
};

bool compareContacts(Contact a, Contact b) {
    return a.name < b.name;  // Sort contacts by name
}

int main() {
    vector<Contact> addressBook;

    // Add some contacts
```

```cpp
    addressBook.push_back({"Alice",    "123-456-
7890"});
    addressBook.push_back({"Bob",       "987-654-
3210"});
    addressBook.push_back({"Charlie",  "555-555-
5555"});

    // Sort contacts by name using quicksort (via
std::sort)
    sort(addressBook.begin(), addressBook.end(),
compareContacts);

    // Display sorted contacts
    cout << "Sorted Address Book: " << endl;
    for (const auto& contact : addressBook) {
        cout << contact.name << ": " <<
contact.phoneNumber << endl;
    }

    // Search for a contact
    string searchName = "Bob";
    auto it = find_if(addressBook.begin(),
addressBook.end(), [&searchName](const Contact&
c) {
        return c.name == searchName;
    });

    if (it != addressBook.end()) {
```

206

```
        cout << "Found " << searchName << ": " <<
it->phoneNumber << endl;
    } else {
        cout << searchName << " not found." <<
endl;
    }

    return 0;
}
```

Explanation:

- The program allows users to add contacts to the address book, sort them by name using the `std::sort()` algorithm (which internally uses **quick sort**), and search for a contact by name using **linear search** (`find_if()`).
- The `compareContacts()` function is used to compare contacts by name for sorting.

Summary:

By the end of this chapter, you should have a solid understanding of:

- **Sorting algorithms**: Bubble Sort, Merge Sort, and QuickSort, along with their time complexities.

- **Searching algorithms**: Linear Search and Binary Search, and when to use each.

- How to implement a **real-world example**: An **address book** with search and sort features, leveraging both sorting and searching algorithms.

In the next chapter, we will dive into **advanced algorithms**, such as **graph algorithms**, **dynamic programming**, and **greedy algorithms**, to further enhance your problem-solving skills in C++.

CHAPTER 18

ADVANCED C++ PROGRAMMING TECHNIQUES

Smart Pointers and Memory Management

In modern C++ (since C++11), **smart pointers** provide automatic memory management, reducing the risk of memory leaks and dangling pointers. A smart pointer is an object that behaves like a pointer but ensures that the memory it points to is properly managed (i.e., automatically deallocated when no longer needed).

The most commonly used smart pointers in C++ are:

- `std::unique_ptr`: Provides exclusive ownership of a dynamically allocated object. Once a `unique_ptr` goes out of scope, it automatically deletes the object it points to.
- `std::shared_ptr`: Allows multiple smart pointers to share ownership of the same object. The object is deleted when the last `shared_ptr` to it goes out of scope.
- `std::weak_ptr`: A non-owning smart pointer that helps break cycles in a graph of `shared_ptr`s.

Example: Using std::unique_ptr

cpp

```cpp
#include <iostream>
#include <memory>  // For unique_ptr
using namespace std;

class MyClass {
public:
    MyClass() { cout << "MyClass created." << endl; }
    ~MyClass() { cout << "MyClass destroyed." << endl; }
};

int main() {
    // Create a unique_ptr to manage MyClass object
    unique_ptr<MyClass> ptr = make_unique<MyClass>();

    // The object is automatically destroyed when ptr goes out of scope
    return 0;
}
```

Explanation:

- A `std::unique_ptr` manages the lifetime of the `MyClass` object. When `ptr` goes out of scope, it automatically calls the destructor of `MyClass`, ensuring memory is freed.

Example: Using `std::shared_ptr`

cpp

```cpp
#include <iostream>
#include <memory>
using namespace std;

class MyClass {
public:
    MyClass() { cout << "MyClass created." << endl; }
    ~MyClass() { cout << "MyClass destroyed." << endl; }
};

int main() {
    shared_ptr<MyClass>            ptr1          = make_shared<MyClass>();
    cout << "Use count: " << ptr1.use_count() << endl;  // Outputs: 1

    shared_ptr<MyClass> ptr2 = ptr1;   // Share ownership
```

211

```
    cout << "Use count: " << ptr1.use_count() <<
endl;   // Outputs: 2

    return 0;
}
```

Explanation:

- `std::shared_ptr` allows multiple pointers to share ownership of the same object. The object is destroyed when the last `shared_ptr` is out of scope. The `use_count()` function returns the number of `shared_ptrs` managing the object.

Benefits of Smart Pointers:

- Automatic memory management.
- Reduces the risk of memory leaks.
- Helps avoid dangling pointers by automatically deleting objects when no longer needed.

Move Semantics and Rvalue References

Move semantics (introduced in C++11) is a feature that allows resources to be transferred from one object to another without performing a deep . This is particularly useful for optimizing the performance of programs that work with large data structures or objects.

Rvalue References (`&&`)

An **rvalue reference** is a reference that can bind to **rvalues**, which are temporary objects or objects that are about to be destroyed. Rvalue references enable **move semantics**, allowing efficient transfers of resources.

- **Lvalue**: An object that has a persistent address in memory (e.g., a variable).
- **Rvalue**: A temporary object or an object that can be moved (e.g., the result of an expression like `std::vector<int>{}`).

Move Constructor and Move Assignment Operator

A **move constructor** transfers ownership of resources from one object to another without ing the underlying data. Similarly, the **move assignment operator** transfers ownership of resources from one object to another after they have been constructed.

Example: Move Constructor and Move Assignment Operator

cpp

```
#include <iostream>
```

```cpp
#include <vector>
using namespace std;

class MyClass {
private:
    vector<int> data;

public:
    MyClass() = default;

    // Move constructor
    MyClass(MyClass&&    other)    noexcept    :
data(std::move(other.data)) {
        cout << "Move constructor called!" <<
endl;
    }

    // Move assignment operator
    MyClass& operator=(MyClass&& other) noexcept
{
        if (this != &other) {
            data = std::move(other.data);
        }
        cout << "Move assignment operator
called!" << endl;
        return *this;
    }

    void addData(int val) {
```

```cpp
        data.push_back(val);
    }


    void printData() const {
        for (int val : data) {
            cout << val << " ";
        }
        cout << endl;
    }
};


int main() {
    MyClass obj1;
    obj1.addData(10);
    obj1.addData(20);
    obj1.printData();

    MyClass obj2 = std::move(obj1);    // Move
constructor is called
    obj2.printData();

    MyClass obj3;
    obj3 = std::move(obj2);   // Move assignment
operator is called
    obj3.printData();

    return 0;
}
```

Explanation:

- The move constructor transfers ownership of the `data` vector from `obj1` to `obj2`.
- The move assignment operator transfers the ownership from `obj2` to `obj3`.
- `std::move()` is used to indicate that the object can be moved (i.e., ownership of its resources can be transferred).

Benefits of Move Semantics:

- Reduces unnecessary deep copies of objects, improving performance.
- Enables more efficient resource management for temporary objects.

Lambda Expressions and Functional Programming

Lambda expressions, introduced in C++11, provide a concise way to define anonymous functions directly in the body of a function or algorithm. They are often used with algorithms like `std::for_each, std::sort,` or `

A network error occurred. Please check your connection and try again. If this issue persists please contact us through our help center at help.openai.com.

CHAPTER 19

DESIGN PATTERNS IN C++

Introduction to Design Patterns

Design Patterns are reusable solutions to common software design problems. They provide general, repeatable solutions to problems that arise in software design. Design patterns have been widely recognized as best practices in object-oriented programming (OOP) because they offer structured approaches to solve complex design issues in a flexible and maintainable way.

In C++, design patterns are particularly important because they help handle the complexity of large applications and improve code modularity, reusability, and maintainability. The **Gang of Four (GoF)** book, *Design Patterns: Elements of Reusable Object-Oriented Software*, introduced 23 classic design patterns, which are divided into three main categories:

- **Creational Patterns**: Deal with object creation mechanisms, trying to create objects in a manner suitable to the situation.
- **Structural Patterns**: Concerned with how classes and objects are composed to form larger structures.

- **Behavioral Patterns**: Focus on the interaction between objects and the delegation of responsibilities.

In this chapter, we will focus on four key design patterns:

- **Singleton Pattern**
- **Factory Pattern**
- **Observer Pattern**
- **Strategy Pattern**

We will discuss how each of these patterns works and how to implement them in C++.

Common Patterns

1. Singleton Pattern

The **Singleton Pattern** ensures that a class has only one instance and provides a global point of access to that instance. This pattern is useful when you need to control access to shared resources, such as logging or database connections.

- **Key Features**:
    - **Only one instance**: Ensures that a class has only one instance throughout the application.
    - **Global access point**: Provides a global access point to the instance.

Example:

cpp

```cpp
#include <iostream>
using namespace std;

class Singleton {
private:
    static Singleton* instance;

    // Private constructor to prevent multiple instances
    Singleton() {}

public:
    static Singleton* getInstance() {
        if (instance == nullptr) {
            instance = new Singleton();
        }
        return instance;
    }

    void showMessage() {
        cout << "Hello from Singleton!" << endl;
    }
};

// Initialize the static member
Singleton* Singleton::instance = nullptr;
```

```
int main() {
    Singleton*              singleton              =
Singleton::getInstance();
    singleton->showMessage();
    return 0;
}
```

Explanation:

- The `Singleton` class ensures that only one instance of itself can be created by keeping a static pointer to its single instance. The `getInstance()` function provides access to this instance.
- The constructor is **private** to prevent external code from creating instances directly.

2. Factory Pattern

The **Factory Pattern** is a creational pattern used to create objects without specifying the exact class of object that will be created. The Factory Pattern defines an interface for creating objects but leaves the decision of which class to instantiate to subclasses or concrete implementations.

- **Key Features**:
    - **Object creation is centralized**: The Factory provides a central point for object creation.

   o **Encapsulates object instantiation**: The client code does not need to know the exact class being instantiated.

Example:

cpp

```cpp
#include <iostream>
#include <memory>
using namespace std;

// Product interface
class Product {
public:
    virtual void doSomething() = 0;
};

// Concrete Product A
class ProductA : public Product {
public:
    void doSomething() override {
        cout << "ProductA doing something!" << endl;
    }
};

// Concrete Product B
class ProductB : public Product {
```

221

```cpp
public:
    void doSomething() override {
        cout << "ProductB doing something!" <<
endl;
    }
};


// Factory class
class Factory {
public:
    static                    unique_ptr<Product>
createProduct(const string& type) {
        if (type == "A") {
            return make_unique<ProductA>();
        } else if (type == "B") {
            return make_unique<ProductB>();
        } else {
            return nullptr;
        }
    }
};


int main() {
    auto product = Factory::createProduct("A");
    product->doSomething();        //    Outputs:
ProductA doing something!

    return 0;
}
```

Explanation:

- The `Factory` class has a `createProduct()` method that creates objects of type `ProductA` or `ProductB` based on the type passed to it. The client code does not need to know the concrete class being instantiated.
- The client interacts only with the abstract `Product` class, making the code more flexible and easier to maintain.

3. Observer Pattern

The **Observer Pattern** is a behavioral pattern used when an object (the **subject**) needs to notify other objects (the **observers**) of state changes. This pattern is often used in scenarios where one object changes and many other objects need to be updated, such as event handling or a publisher-subscriber system.

- **Key Features**:
  - **One-to-many dependency**: When the subject's state changes, all observers are notified.
  - **Loose coupling**: The subject and observers are decoupled from each other, making the system more flexible.

Example:

cpp

```cpp
#include <iostream>
#include <vector>
#include <string>
using namespace std;

// Observer interface
class Observer {
public:
    virtual void update(const string& message) =
0;
};

// Concrete Observer
class Display : public Observer {
public:
    void update(const string& message) override
{
        cout << "Display received message: " <<
message << endl;
    }
};

// Subject interface
class Subject {
public:
    virtual void addObserver(Observer* observer)
= 0;
    virtual    void    removeObserver(Observer*
observer) = 0;
```

```cpp
    virtual void notifyObservers() = 0;
};


// Concrete Subject
class WeatherStation : public Subject {
private:
    vector<Observer*> observers;
    string weatherUpdate;

public:
    void setWeatherUpdate(const string& update)
{
        weatherUpdate = update;
        notifyObservers();
    }


    void    addObserver(Observer*    observer)
override {
        observers.push_back(observer);
    }


    void    removeObserver(Observer*    observer)
override {

observers.erase(remove(observers.begin(),
observers.end(), observer), observers.end());
    }


    void notifyObservers() override {
```

```
        for (auto observer : observers) {
            observer->update(weatherUpdate);
        }
    }
};

int main() {
    WeatherStation station;
    Display display1, display2;

    station.addObserver(&display1);
    station.addObserver(&display2);

    station.setWeatherUpdate("Sunny");
    station.setWeatherUpdate("Rainy");

    return 0;
}
```

Explanation:

- The `WeatherStation` class is the subject that holds a list of observers (displays). When the weather changes, it notifies all registered observers with the new update.
- The `Display` class implements the `Observer` interface and updates itself when the weather changes.

4. Strategy Pattern

The **Strategy Pattern** is a behavioral design pattern that defines a family of algorithms, encapsulates each one, and makes them interchangeable. It allows the algorithm to be selected at runtime, making the code more flexible and easier to extend.

- **Key Features**:
  - **Interchangeable strategies**: The context can switch between different algorithms dynamically.
  - **Open for extension, closed for modification**: New strategies can be added without modifying the context.

Example:

cpp

```cpp
#include <iostream>
#include <memory>
using namespace std;

// Strategy interface
class SortStrategy {
public:
    virtual void sort() const = 0;
};

// Concrete Strategy A
```

```cpp
class QuickSort : public SortStrategy {
public:
    void sort() const override {
        cout << "Sorting using QuickSort." <<
endl;
    }
};


// Concrete Strategy B
class MergeSort : public SortStrategy {
public:
    void sort() const override {
        cout << "Sorting using MergeSort." <<
endl;
    }
};


// Context
class SortContext {
private:
    unique_ptr<SortStrategy> strategy;

public:
    void    setStrategy(unique_ptr<SortStrategy>
newStrategy) {
        strategy = move(newStrategy);
    }

    void executeSort() const {
```

```
        strategy->sort();
    }
};

int main() {
    SortContext context;
```

```
context.setStrategy(make_unique<QuickSort>());
    context.executeSort();   // Outputs: Sorting
using QuickSort.
```

```
context.setStrategy(make_unique<MergeSort>());
    context.executeSort();   // Outputs: Sorting
using MergeSort.

    return 0;
}
```

Explanation:

- The SortContext class uses a SortStrategy to perform sorting. The strategy can be changed dynamically using the setStrategy() method.
- The QuickSort and MergeSort classes are concrete strategies that implement the SortStrategy interface.
- The context uses the appropriate strategy at runtime to perform the sorting operation.

229

Real-World Example: Applying the Observer Pattern to a Weather Station Simulation

In this section, we've already demonstrated how to use the **Observer Pattern** in a simple weather station simulation. This pattern can be used in real-world scenarios such as:

- **News aggregators** where multiple components (websites, apps, etc.) listen to a central news feed.
- **Stock market applications** where users subscribe to price updates.

The Observer Pattern makes these systems flexible and scalable because you can add or remove observers without affecting the core logic.

Summary:

By the end of this chapter, you should:

- Understand and be able to implement key **design patterns** in C++:
  - **Singleton Pattern** for ensuring one instance of a class.

- o **Factory Pattern** for object creation without specifying exact types.
- o **Observer Pattern** for a one-to-many relationship between objects.
- o **Strategy Pattern** for dynamically changing algorithms.
- Be able to apply design patterns in real-world applications to solve complex problems in a clean and maintainable way.

In the next chapter, we will explore **multithreading** and **concurrency** in C++ to build more efficient and scalable applications.

CHAPTER 20

NETWORK PROGRAMMING IN C++

Introduction to Network Programming

Network programming refers to writing software that enables communication between different devices over a network. It involves creating programs that allow machines to exchange data, interact, and communicate with each other. In C++, network programming is commonly done using **sockets**. A socket is an endpoint for communication between two machines, enabling the exchange of data across a network.

Network programming is essential for creating client-server applications, such as:

- **Web servers**
- **Chat applications**
- **File transfer protocols**
- **Online games**

In this chapter, we will explore the basics of **socket programming** in C++ and implement a simple chat application that demonstrates how data is transmitted between a client and server using sockets.

Creating Servers and Clients with Sockets

In network programming, the **client** is a program that connects to the **server** to send and receive data. The **server** listens for incoming client connections and responds with appropriate data.

Socket Basics:

- **Socket**: A software endpoint that establishes a communication channel for network communication.
- **Port**: A communication endpoint used by a server to listen for incoming client requests. Ports are identified by numbers, such as 80 for HTTP or 8080 for web servers.
- **IP Address**: Identifies a device on the network. It is essential for addressing the devices involved in communication.

Creating a Server in C++

The server's job is to wait for incoming connections from clients, process the request, and send a response. Here's how you can create a basic server using sockets in C++:

Steps to create a basic server:

1. **Create a socket** using `socket()` function.
2. **Bind** the socket to an IP address and a port using `bind()`.
3. **Listen** for incoming connections using `listen()`.
4. **Accept** connections from clients using `accept()`.
5. **Read/write data** using `read()` and `write()`.
6. **Close** the socket when finished.

Basic Server Code Example (Using TCP Sockets):

cpp

```cpp
#include <iostream>
#include <sys/socket.h>
#include <netinet/in.h>
#include <unistd.h>
#include <string.h>
using namespace std;

#define PORT 8080  // Port number for the server
to listen on

int main() {
    int server_fd, new_socket;
    struct sockaddr_in address;
    int addrlen = sizeof(address);

    // Create socket
```

```cpp
    if    ((server_fd    =    socket(AF_INET,
SOCK_STREAM, 0)) == 0) {
        perror("Socket failed");
        exit(EXIT_FAILURE);
    }

    // Setup server address structure
    address.sin_family = AF_INET;
    address.sin_addr.s_addr = INADDR_ANY;
    address.sin_port = htons(PORT);

    // Bind the socket to the port
    if    (bind(server_fd,    (struct    sockaddr
*)&address, sizeof(address)) < 0) {
        perror("Bind failed");
        exit(EXIT_FAILURE);
    }

    // Listen for incoming connections
    if (listen(server_fd, 3) < 0) {
        perror("Listen failed");
        exit(EXIT_FAILURE);
    }

    cout << "Server is listening on port " <<
PORT << "...\n";

    // Accept incoming connections
```

```cpp
    if ((new_socket = accept(server_fd, (struct
sockaddr *)&address, (socklen_t*)&addrlen)) < 0)
{
        perror("Accept failed");
        exit(EXIT_FAILURE);
    }

    // Send message to the client
    const char* message = "Hello from server!";
    send(new_socket, message, strlen(message),
0);
    cout << "Message sent to client.\n";

    // Close the socket
    close(new_socket);
    close(server_fd);

    return 0;
}
```

Explanation:

- The server creates a socket using the `socket()` function, binds it to a port (`8080`), listens for incoming connections, and accepts them when they arrive.
- Once a connection is established, the server sends a message to the client, then closes the connection.

Creating a Client in C++

A client connects to the server, sends requests, and waits for responses. The basic steps for creating a client are:

1. **Create a socket** using `socket()`.
2. **Connect** the client to the server using `connect()`.
3. **Send/Receive data** using `send()` and `recv()`.
4. **Close the socket** when done.

Basic Client Code Example:

cpp

```cpp
#include <iostream>
#include <sys/socket.h>
#include <netinet/in.h>
#include <unistd.h>
#include <cstring>
using namespace std;

#define PORT 8080

int main() {
    int sock = 0;
    struct sockaddr_in server_addr;
    char buffer[1024] = {0};

    // Create socket
```

```cpp
    if ((sock = socket(AF_INET, SOCK_STREAM, 0))
< 0) {
        perror("Socket failed");
        exit(EXIT_FAILURE);
    }

    // Setup server address structure
    server_addr.sin_family = AF_INET;
    server_addr.sin_port = htons(PORT);

    // Convert IP address from text to binary
form
    if     (inet_pton(AF_INET,     "127.0.0.1",
&server_addr.sin_addr) <= 0) {
        perror("Invalid    address/Address    not
supported");
        exit(EXIT_FAILURE);
    }

    // Connect to the server
    if    (connect(sock,    (struct    sockaddr
*)&server_addr, sizeof(server_addr)) < 0) {
        perror("Connection failed");
        exit(EXIT_FAILURE);
    }

    // Read the server's response
    read(sock, buffer, sizeof(buffer));
```

```
    cout << "Message from server: " << buffer <<
endl;

    // Close the socket
    close(sock);

    return 0;
}
```

Explanation:

- The client creates a socket, connects to the server at IP address 127.0.0.1 and port 8080, and then reads the message sent by the server.

Handling Data Transmission in C++

Once the client-server connection is established, data can be exchanged using **TCP sockets**. You can send data using the send() function and receive data using the recv() or read() functions, depending on the operating system.

- **send()**: Sends data over a socket.
- **recv() / read()**: Receives data from a socket.
- **close()**: Closes the socket when done.

Both client and server should handle data transmission carefully:

- **Buffers**: You typically use buffers (character arrays) to send or receive data. The size of the buffer should be large enough to hold the expected data.

- **Error Handling**: Always check for errors after each socket operation, such as `send()`, `recv()`, or `accept()`.

Real-World Example: A Simple Chat Application Using Sockets

Let's implement a simple **chat application** that allows the client and server to exchange messages in real-time. We will use the concepts from previous sections (servers, clients, data transmission) to build a simple system where the server and client can send messages back and forth.

Chat Server Code:

cpp

```cpp
#include <iostream>
#include <sys/socket.h>
#include <netinet/in.h>
#include <unistd.h>
#include <string.h>
using namespace std;

#define PORT 8080
```

```cpp
int main() {
    int server_fd, new_socket;
    struct sockaddr_in address;
    int addrlen = sizeof(address);
    char buffer[1024] = {0};

    if    ((server_fd    =    socket(AF_INET,
SOCK_STREAM, 0)) == 0) {
        perror("Socket failed");
        exit(EXIT_FAILURE);
    }

    address.sin_family = AF_INET;
    address.sin_addr.s_addr = INADDR_ANY;
    address.sin_port = htons(PORT);

    if    (bind(server_fd,    (struct    sockaddr
*)&address, sizeof(address)) < 0) {
        perror("Bind failed");
        exit(EXIT_FAILURE);
    }

    if (listen(server_fd, 3) < 0) {
        perror("Listen failed");
        exit(EXIT_FAILURE);
    }

    cout << "Server listening on port " << PORT
<< "...\n";
```

```cpp
    if ((new_socket = accept(server_fd, (struct
sockaddr *)&address, (socklen_t*)&addrlen)) < 0)
{
        perror("Accept failed");
        exit(EXIT_FAILURE);
    }

    while (true) {
        read(new_socket,                    buffer,
sizeof(buffer));
        cout << "Client: " << buffer << endl;
        memset(buffer, 0, sizeof(buffer));

        cout << "Server: ";
        string msg;
        getline(cin, msg);
        send(new_socket,              msg.c_str(),
msg.length(), 0);
    }

    close(new_socket);
    close(server_fd);

    return 0;
}
```

Chat Client Code:

cpp

```cpp
#include <iostream>
#include <sys/socket.h>
#include <netinet/in.h>
#include <unistd.h>
#include <cstring>
using namespace std;

#define PORT 8080

int main() {
    int sock = 0;
    struct sockaddr_in server_addr;
    char buffer[1024] = {0};

    if ((sock = socket(AF_INET, SOCK_STREAM, 0)) < 0) {
        perror("Socket failed");
        exit(EXIT_FAILURE);
    }

    server_addr.sin_family = AF_INET;
    server_addr.sin_port = htons(PORT);

    if    (inet_pton(AF_INET,    "127.0.0.1",
&server_addr.sin_addr) <= 0) {
        perror("Invalid    address/Address    not
supported");
        exit(EXIT_FAILURE);
    }
```

```
    if      (connect(sock,      (struct      sockaddr
*)&server_addr, sizeof(server_addr)) < 0) {
        perror("Connection failed");
        exit(EXIT_FAILURE);
    }

    while (true) {
        cout << "Client: ";
        string msg;
        getline(cin, msg);
        send(sock,   msg.c_str(),   msg.length(),
0);

        read(sock, buffer, sizeof(buffer));
        cout << "Server: " << buffer << endl;
        memset(buffer, 0, sizeof(buffer));
    }

    close(sock);

    return 0;
}
```

Explanation:

- **Server**: The server listens on port 8080 for incoming client connections. Once a connection is established, it enters a loop to receive messages from the client and send responses back.

- **Client**: The client connects to the server at `127.0.0.1` (localhost). It then enters a loop to send messages to the server and print the server's responses.

The **chat application** demonstrates basic real-time communication using TCP sockets. Both the server and client can send and receive messages in a continuous loop, creating an interactive chat system.

Summary:

By the end of this chapter, you should:

- Understand the basics of **network programming** in C++ using **sockets**.
- Know how to create a **server** and **client** that can exchange data using TCP sockets.
- Learn how to handle **data transmission** using `send()`, `recv()`, and `read()` functions.
- Have implemented a **real-world example**: A simple **chat application** using sockets for communication between client and server.

In the next chapter, we will delve into **advanced topics in network programming**, such as **multi-threaded servers, UDP sockets**, and **data serialization** for more complex applications.

CHAPTER 21

BUILDING A C++ APPLICATION: FROM CONCEPT TO EXECUTION

Defining Project Scope and Planning

When building a C++ application, the first and most crucial step is to define the **project scope** and **plan** how the application will be developed. This process ensures that the project remains manageable, within budget (in terms of time and resources), and meets the desired objectives.

Steps to Define the Project Scope:

1. **Understand the Requirements**:
   o What problem does the application solve?
   o Who are the users, and what are their expectations?
   o What functionality does the application need?

2. **Outline Key Features**:
   o Create a list of core features, such as login systems, file I/O, database management, user interfaces, and more.

o Define whether your application will be a command-line program or a graphical user interface (GUI) application.

3. **Identify Dependencies**:

o What external libraries or frameworks will be needed? For example, if you are building a GUI, libraries like **Qt** or **SFML** might be necessary.

4. **Define Milestones**:

o Break the project into smaller, manageable tasks or milestones. Each milestone should represent a functional part of the project (e.g., setting up version control, implementing a feature, testing).

5. **Estimate Time and Resources**:

o Estimate how long each milestone will take to complete.

o Identify the required resources, including development tools, hardware, and testing environments.

Example: Planning a Simple C++ Desktop Application

Let's consider the example of building a **To-Do List** application:

- **Scope**: A desktop application to manage tasks, with features like adding, removing, and displaying tasks.
- **Key Features**: Task management (add, remove, display), user interface, data storage.

- **Dependencies**: We'll use **Qt** for the GUI and **JSON** to store tasks.
- **Milestones**:
  1. Setup version control and environment.
  2. Implement task management logic.
  3. Create the user interface.
  4. Implement file I/O for task persistence.
  5. Test and debug.

Using Version Control with Git

Version control is a crucial part of software development. It allows multiple developers (or a single developer) to track changes, collaborate, and revert to earlier versions of the code when necessary. **Git** is the most widely used version control system, and it integrates well with platforms like **GitHub**, **GitLab**, and **Bitbucket**.

Basic Git Workflow:

1. **Initialize a Git Repository**:
   o Start by creating a new Git repository in your project directory using `git init`.

   bash

   ```
   git init
   ```

2. **Staging Changes**:

    o   Before committing changes, you need to stage them using `git add`. This allows you to select which changes will be included in the next commit.

bash

```
git add <file>   # Add a specific file
git add .        # Add all changed files
```

3. **Committing Changes**:

    o   After staging the changes, commit them with a message describing what was changed.

bash

```
git commit -m "Initial commit with basic structure"
```

4. **Pushing to Remote Repository**:

    o   To share your changes with others or store them remotely, push your commits to a remote repository (e.g., GitHub).

bash

```
git push origin main
```

5. **Pulling Changes**:

   o To retrieve the latest changes from a remote
   repository, use `git pull`.

bash

```
git pull origin main
```

6. **Branching and Merging**:

   o You can create branches to work on different
   features without affecting the main branch (`main`
   or `master`). Once the work is done, you can
   merge the branch back into the main branch.

bash

```
git branch new-feature    # Create a new
branch
git checkout new-feature  # Switch to the
new branch
git merge new-feature  # Merge the feature
branch into main
```

Best Practices:

- **Commit frequently**: Make commits at logical points to
  document progress.
- **Write meaningful commit messages**: This helps both
  you and your collaborators understand what was changed.

251

- **Use branches**: For working on new features or bug fixes, create a separate branch to keep the main branch stable.

Compiling and Debugging

When working with C++, **compiling** and **debugging** are essential processes for turning your source code into executable software and ensuring it works correctly.

Compiling C++ Code:

In C++, the compiler translates your source code into machine code that can be executed. Common C++ compilers include:

- **GCC (GNU Compiler Collection)**
- **Clang**
- **Microsoft Visual C++**

To compile a C++ program, you typically run the following command in the terminal:

```bash
g++ -o my_program my_program.cpp   # GCC example
```

This command compiles the `my_program.cpp` source file into an executable named `my_program`.

Debugging:

Debugging helps identify and fix bugs in your program. Modern IDEs (like **Qt Creator** or **Visual Studio**) provide built-in debuggers, but you can also use standalone debuggers like **GDB** (GNU Debugger).

Some common debugging techniques:

- **Set breakpoints**: Stop execution at specific points to inspect the program's state.
- **Step through code**: Execute code line-by-line to observe the flow of execution.
- **Inspect variables**: View the values of variables at different points in the program to identify issues.

Example (using GDB):

1. Compile with debugging symbols:

```bash
```

```bash
g++ -g -o my_program my_program.cpp
```

2. Start GDB:

```bash
```

```bash
gdb ./my_program
```

3. Set breakpoints and run the program:

```bash

break main
run
```

Real-World Example: Building and Deploying a Simple Desktop Application

Let's implement a **To-Do List** desktop application using **Qt** (a C++ framework for GUI development). We'll cover the following steps:

1. **Design the application**: Outline the features (task list, add/remove tasks).
2. **Write the application code**: Implement the functionality using C++ and Qt.
3. **Compile and test**: Compile the application and test it for bugs.
4. **Deploy the application**: Package and deploy the application.

Step 1: Designing the Application

Our **To-Do List** application will have:

- A **list view** to display tasks.

254

- Buttons to **add** and **remove** tasks.
- The ability to **save** the tasks to a file.

Step 2: Writing the Code

Main Window (Qt):

cpp

```
#include <QApplication>
#include <QWidget>
#include <QPushButton>
#include <QListWidget>
#include <QLineEdit>
#include <QVBoxLayout>
#include <QFile>
#include <QTextStream>
#include <QMessageBox>

class TodoApp : public QWidget {
    Q_OBJECT

public:
    TodoApp() {
        QVBoxLayout*     layout     =     new
QVBoxLayout(this);

        taskInput = new QLineEdit(this);
```

```cpp
        taskInput->setPlaceholderText("Enter
task...");
        layout->addWidget(taskInput);

        taskList = new QListWidget(this);
        layout->addWidget(taskList);

        addButton = new QPushButton("Add Task",
this);
        layout->addWidget(addButton);

        removeButton = new QPushButton("Remove
Task", this);
        layout->addWidget(removeButton);

        connect(addButton,
&QPushButton::clicked, this, &TodoApp::addTask);
        connect(removeButton,
&QPushButton::clicked,                    this,
&TodoApp::removeTask);

        setLayout(layout);
        setWindowTitle("To-Do List");
        resize(300, 400);

        loadTasks();
    }

private slots:
```

```cpp
void addTask() {
    QString task = taskInput->text();
    if (!task.isEmpty()) {
        taskList->addItem(task);
        taskInput->clear();
        saveTasks();
    } else {
        QMessageBox::warning(this,     "Input
Error", "Please enter a task.");
    }
}

void removeTask() {
    QListWidgetItem*   item   =   taskList->currentItem();
    if (item) {
        delete item;
        saveTasks();
    } else {
        QMessageBox::warning(this,
"Selection   Error",   "Please   select   a   task   to
remove.");
    }
}

void loadTasks() {
    QFile file("tasks.txt");
    if (file.open(QIODevice::ReadOnly)) {
        QTextStream in(&file);
```

```cpp
        while (!in.atEnd()) {
            QString task = in.readLine();
            taskList->addItem(task);
        }
        file.close();
    }
}

void saveTasks() {
    QFile file("tasks.txt");
    if (file.open(QIODevice::WriteOnly)) {
        QTextStream out(&file);
        for (int i = 0; i < taskList->count(); ++i) {
            out << taskList->item(i)->text() << "\n";
        }
        file.close();
    }
}

private:
    QLineEdit* taskInput;
    QListWidget* taskList;
    QPushButton* addButton;
    QPushButton* removeButton;
};

int main(int argc, char *argv[]) {
```

```
QApplication app(argc, argv);
TodoApp window;
window.show();
return app.exec();
}
```

Step 3: Compile and Test the Application

- Install **Qt Creator** or use your preferred C++ IDE to compile the code.
- Run the application to ensure all features (adding, removing, saving, and loading tasks) work as expected.

Step 4: Deploy the Application

- For **Windows**, you can use Qt's **windeployqt** tool to package your application.
- For **Linux**, package your application using tools like **CMake** or **Make** and distribute the binaries.

Summary:

By the end of this chapter, you should:

- Understand how to define the **project scope** and plan a C++ application from concept to execution.

- Be familiar with **version control** using **Git** to manage your code.
- Know how to **compile and debug** C++ code using common tools.
- Have created and deployed a **simple desktop application** (To-Do List) using **Qt**.

In the next chapter, we will explore **advanced deployment techniques**, such as creating **cross-platform applications** and **distributing applications to end users**.

CHAPTER 22

C++ FOR GAME DEVELOPMENT

Introduction to Game Development in C++

C++ has long been a dominant language in game development due to its performance, flexibility, and control over system resources. Whether you are developing high-performance games for consoles, PC, or mobile platforms, C++ provides the necessary features for efficient memory management, low-latency systems, and real-time processing.

In this chapter, we will explore the world of **C++ game development**, including:

- Game engines that integrate with C++.
- Libraries for working with 2D and 3D games.
- A real-world example of creating a simple 2D game using a popular game library.

Game development often involves a combination of various concepts, including:

- **Graphics**: Rendering 2D or 3D images.

- **Physics**: Simulating motion, collision, and other physical phenomena.
- **Input Handling**: Managing user inputs such as keyboard and mouse events.
- **Sound**: Adding audio to enhance the user experience.

Let's dive into some of the most important aspects of C++ game development.

Game Engines like Unreal Engine and C++ Integration

1. Unreal Engine

Unreal Engine is one of the most widely used game engines in the industry. It provides a high-performance engine for creating complex 3D games, simulations, and virtual reality (VR) experiences. Unreal Engine supports C++ natively and also uses its own visual scripting language called **Blueprints**, which makes it accessible to both programmers and non-programmers.

- **C++ Integration in Unreal Engine**:
    - Unreal Engine's core framework is written in C++, and it exposes a powerful API that allows developers to customize and extend the engine.
    - Game logic, physics, and AI behavior can be scripted using C++.

- o Unreal provides a real-time, interactive development environment, where you can test your game while developing it, improving productivity and iteration speed.
- **Why Use Unreal Engine with C++?**:
  - o Unreal is ideal for high-fidelity 3D games and supports modern graphics technologies like **ray tracing** and **global illumination**.
  - o C++ allows you to optimize performance-critical parts of your game for high-quality experiences.

Example: In Unreal Engine, you can use C++ to manage game objects, character behavior, and other key elements. Here's an example of defining a simple actor (an object in the game world) in C++.

cpp

```cpp
#include "GameFramework/Actor.h"
#include "MyActor.generated.h"

UCLASS()
class MYGAME_API AMyActor : public AActor {
    GENERATED_BODY()

public:
    AMyActor();
```

```
protected:
    virtual void BeginPlay() override;

public:
    virtual void Tick(float DeltaTime) override;
};
```

In this example, AMyActor is a C++ class representing an actor in the Unreal Engine world, and it implements BeginPlay and Tick, which are called during the game loop to handle initialization and update tasks.

---

2. Unity vs Unreal for C++ Developers

While **Unity** primarily uses **C#**, **Unreal Engine** uses C++ as its primary programming language, making it a more natural fit for developers who want to leverage the power of C++ in game development. C++ gives developers access to low-level memory management, advanced performance optimization, and deep integration with the engine's functionality, making it ideal for AAA game development.

Game Libraries for 2D/3D Game Development

If you want to develop simpler 2D or 3D games, or if you prefer not to use a full-fledged game engine like Unreal, there are several

game libraries that you can use to manage graphics, input, sound, and more.

1. SDL (Simple DirectMedia Layer)

SDL is a lightweight, cross-platform library used for developing 2D games. It provides low-level access to video, audio, input devices, and timers, making it a good choice for developers who need more control over their game's performance.

Key Features:

- Handles **graphics rendering** with support for 2D images, pixel manipulation, and even simple 3D using OpenGL.
- Supports **audio** playback, including sound effects and music.
- Provides event handling for **keyboard, mouse, and joystick** input.
- Easy to integrate with **OpenGL** or **Vulkan** for 3D graphics.

2. SFML (Simple and Fast Multimedia Library)

SFML is another lightweight and easy-to-use multimedia library for 2D game development. SFML simplifies the process of working with graphics, sound, and input. It is object-oriented, making it easier to use and more intuitive than SDL.

Key Features:

- Provides an object-oriented API for **graphics, sound, network, and input**.
- Uses **OpenGL** for rendering, which can be extended for more complex 3D games.
- Easy-to-use and great for rapid development of 2D games.

Real-World Example: Creating a Simple 2D Game Using SDL or SFML

Let's walk through creating a **simple 2D game** using **SFML**. We will create a game where a player-controlled character can move around the screen, represented as a square.

Step 1: Install SFML

Before you start, you need to install SFML on your system. You can download SFML from the official website: SFML Downloads.

For example, on Linux, you can install it with:

```bash

sudo apt-get install libsfml-dev
```

Step 2: Code the 2D Game

Game Loop: The basic structure of a game is a loop that continually updates the game state and renders frames to the screen.

cpp

```
#include <SFML/Graphics.hpp>

int main() {
    // Create a window
    sf::RenderWindow  window(sf::VideoMode(800,
600), "Simple 2D Game");

    // Create a player object (a simple
rectangle)
    sf::RectangleShape  player(sf::Vector2f(50,
50));
    player.setFillColor(sf::Color::Green);
    player.setPosition(375,  275);   // Start
position

    // Set up the game clock
    sf::Clock clock;

    // Game loop
    while (window.isOpen()) {
        sf::Time deltaTime = clock.restart();
```

267

```
sf::Event event;

while (window.pollEvent(event)) {
    if (event.type == sf::Event::Closed)
        window.close();
}

// Handle player movement
if
(sf::Keyboard::isKeyPressed(sf::Keyboard::Left)
) {
        player.move(-200.0f                    *
deltaTime.asSeconds(), 0);  // Move left
    }
    if
(sf::Keyboard::isKeyPressed(sf::Keyboard::Right
)) {
        player.move(200.0f                     *
deltaTime.asSeconds(), 0);  // Move right
    }
    if
(sf::Keyboard::isKeyPressed(sf::Keyboard::Up)) {
        player.move(0,          -200.0f        *
deltaTime.asSeconds());  // Move up
    }
    if
(sf::Keyboard::isKeyPressed(sf::Keyboard::Down)
) {
```

```
        player.move(0,           200.0f        *
deltaTime.asSeconds());  // Move down
        }

        // Clear the screen
        window.clear(sf::Color::Black);

        // Draw the player
        window.draw(player);

        // Display the contents of the window
        window.display();
    }

    return 0;
}
```

Explanation:

- **SFML Window**: The `sf::RenderWindow` object creates a window where the game is rendered.
- **Player Object**: We use `sf::RectangleShape` to represent the player. The player can be moved using the arrow keys.
- **Game Loop**: The main game loop processes events, handles input, updates the game state, and renders the screen. The `sf::Clock` object tracks the time and ensures smooth movement by using `deltaTime`.

Step 3: Compile and Run the Game

To compile the program, you'll need to link against the SFML libraries. The compilation command might look like this (on Linux):

```bash
```

```
g++ -o simple_game simple_game.cpp -lsfml-graphics -lsfml-window -lsfml-system
```

Then, run the game:

```bash
```

```
./simple_game
```

Extending the Game

Once you have the basic framework, you can extend the game with additional features such as:

- **Collision detection**: Add obstacles and detect when the player collides with them.
- **Score tracking**: Keep track of the player's score and display it on the screen.
- **Game states**: Implement menus, pause screens, and game over logic.

Summary:

By the end of this chapter, you should:

- Understand the fundamentals of **C++ game development**.
- Be familiar with popular game engines like **Unreal Engine** and their integration with C++.
- Know how to use **game libraries** like **SFML** to build 2D games.
- Have implemented a **real-world example** of a **2D game** using **SFML**, where you can control a character and move it around the screen.

In the next chapter, we will explore more **advanced game development concepts**, including **3D game development**, **game physics**, and integrating **AI behaviors** in games.

CHAPTER 23

TESTING IN C++

Unit testing is an essential practice in software development that helps ensure the correctness of code by testing individual components (functions, classes) in isolation. C++ offers several frameworks for unit testing, with **Google Test** and **Catch2** being two of the most popular ones.

Google Test

Google Test (also known as **gtest**) is an open-source unit testing framework for C++. It provides a rich set of assertion macros, test fixtures, and a test runner to help automate the testing process. It is widely used in the C++ community, and it integrates well with build systems like **CMake**.

- **Key Features**:
  - Supports a wide range of assertions.
  - Allows parameterized tests.
  - Provides test fixtures for setting up and tearing down test environments.
  - Excellent reporting and debugging capabilities.

Installation: To use Google Test, you'll need to include it in your project by either downloading the source code or using a package manager like **vcpkg** or **Conan**.

Catch2

Catch2 is another open-source unit testing framework that is lightweight and easy to integrate. It's known for its simplicity and ease of use, making it a great choice for developers who want to write tests with minimal setup.

- **Key Features**:
    - Single-header library, making it easy to integrate.
    - Rich set of assertions and matchers.
    - Supports tests in the form of a single function or test cases with multiple checks.
    - Simple syntax and expressive error messages.

Installation: Catch2 is a header-only library, meaning you can directly include the header file in your project.

Writing Unit Tests in C++

Unit tests are designed to validate that individual units of code (usually functions or methods) perform as expected. The goal is to isolate a unit of work and test it independently from other parts of the system.

Basic Unit Test Structure:

Unit tests typically consist of:

1. **Test Case**: A function that contains one or more assertions to verify the behavior of the code.
2. **Setup**: Preparing the test environment, including creating test objects or mocking dependencies.
3. **Tear down**: Cleaning up after the test.

Example with Google Test:

Let's write a simple unit test for a class that adds two integers.

Code to be tested:

cpp

```cpp
class Calculator {
public:
    int add(int a, int b) {
        return a + b;
    }
};
```

Google Test Unit Test:

cpp

```cpp
#include <gtest/gtest.h>
#include "Calculator.h"  // Include the class we
are testing

// Test case for the add function
TEST(CalculatorTest, AddTest) {
    Calculator calc;
    EXPECT_EQ(calc.add(3, 4), 7);  // Assert that
3 + 4 equals 7
    EXPECT_EQ(calc.add(-3, 4), 1);   // Assert
that -3 + 4 equals 1
    EXPECT_EQ(calc.add(-3, -4), -7); // Assert
that -3 + -4 equals -7
}

int main(int argc, char **argv) {
    ::testing::InitGoogleTest(&argc, argv);
    return RUN_ALL_TESTS();
}
```

Explanation:

- **TEST()** macro defines a test case. The first argument is the test suite name (CalculatorTest), and the second is the name of the test (AddTest).

- **EXPECT_EQ()** is used to compare the result of the add() function with the expected value.

- **RUN_ALL_TESTS()** runs all the tests that have been defined.

275

Running the Test:

bash

```
g++ -std=c++11 -lgtest -lgtest_main -pthread
your_test_file.cpp -o test
./test
```

Example with Catch2:

Here's how to write the same unit test using Catch2.

Catch2 Unit Test:

cpp

```
#define CATCH_CONFIG_MAIN
#include <catch2/catch.hpp>
#include "Calculator.h"

TEST_CASE("Addition of two numbers", "[add]") {
    Calculator calc;
    REQUIRE(calc.add(3, 4) == 7);  // Assert that
3 + 4 equals 7
    REQUIRE(calc.add(-3, 4) == 1);  // Assert
that -3 + 4 equals 1
    REQUIRE(calc.add(-3, -4) == -7); // Assert
that -3 + -4 equals -7
}
```

Explanation:

- **REQUIRE()** is used for assertions in Catch2, similar to `EXPECT_EQ()` in Google Test.
- The `CATCH_CONFIG_MAIN` macro automatically provides the main function, so no need to write `main()` yourself.

Running the Test:

```bash

g++ -std=c++11 your_test_file.cpp -o test -lCatch2
./test
```

Test-Driven Development (TDD)

Test-Driven Development (TDD) is a software development methodology in which tests are written before the code. The typical TDD cycle follows three simple steps:

1. **Write a Test**: Write a test that defines a function or improvements to a function.
2. **Run the Test**: Run the test, which should fail since the functionality is not yet implemented.
3. **Write the Code**: Write the minimal amount of code necessary to pass the test.

4. **Refactor**: Clean up the code while ensuring the test still passes.

5. **Repeat**: Continue this cycle for each feature.

TDD Example: Let's implement a basic calculator that supports addition and subtraction using TDD:

1. **Write the test** for subtraction:

cpp

```
TEST(CalculatorTest, SubtractTest) {
    Calculator calc;
    EXPECT_EQ(calc.subtract(7, 4), 3);  // 7 - 4
= 3
    EXPECT_EQ(calc.subtract(-3, 4), -7); // -3 -
4 = -7
}
```

2. **Run the test** (this test will fail since the subtract() function is not implemented yet).

3. **Write the subtract() function** in the Calculator class:

cpp

```
class Calculator {
public:
    int add(int a, int b) {
```

```cpp
        return a + b;
    }

    int subtract(int a, int b) {
        return a - b;
    }
};
```

4. **Run the tests** again to ensure that the new function works.

5. **Refactor** the code as needed, ensuring the tests still pass.

Real-World Example: Writing Unit Tests for a Class that Handles File Operations

Let's write unit tests for a class that reads and writes data to a file. We'll test the `FileHandler` class, which has functions for reading and writing to a file.

FileHandler Class:

cpp

```cpp
#include <iostream>
#include <fstream>
#include <string>
using namespace std;

class FileHandler {
public:
```

```cpp
    bool  writeToFile(const   string&   filename,
const string& content) {
        ofstream outFile(filename);
        if (!outFile.is_open()) {
            return false;
        }
        outFile << content;
        outFile.close();
        return true;
    }

    string readFromFile(const string& filename)
{
        ifstream inFile(filename);
        if (!inFile.is_open()) {
            return "";
        }
        string
content((istreambuf_iterator<char>(inFile)),
istreambuf_iterator<char>());
        inFile.close();
        return content;
    }
};
```

Unit Test for FileHandler (Using Google Test):

cpp

```cpp
#include <gtest/gtest.h>
#include "FileHandler.h"
```

280

```cpp
#include <fstream>

TEST(FileHandlerTest, WriteToFile) {
    FileHandler fileHandler;

EXPECT_TRUE(fileHandler.writeToFile("test.txt",
"Hello, C++!"));

    // Verify file content
    ifstream inFile("test.txt");
    string content;
    getline(inFile, content);
    inFile.close();
    EXPECT_EQ(content, "Hello, C++!");
}

TEST(FileHandlerTest, ReadFromFile) {
    FileHandler fileHandler;
    fileHandler.writeToFile("test.txt",    "Test
reading");

    string              content              =
fileHandler.readFromFile("test.txt");
    EXPECT_EQ(content, "Test reading");
}

TEST(FileHandlerTest, ReadFromNonExistentFile) {
    FileHandler fileHandler;
```

281

```
    string              content              =
fileHandler.readFromFile("nonexistent.txt");
    EXPECT_EQ(content, "");
}
```

Explanation:

- The first test, **WriteToFile**, verifies that the `writeToFile()` function correctly writes content to the file and that the content matches what was written.
- The second test, **ReadFromFile**, tests the `readFromFile()` function by verifying that it reads the correct content.
- The third test, **ReadFromNonExistentFile**, tests how the function handles the case where the file does not exist (it should return an empty string).

Running the Unit Tests:

bash

```
g++ -std=c++11 -lgtest -lgtest_main -pthread
filehandler_test.cpp -o filehandler_test
./filehandler_test
```

Summary:

By the end of this chapter, you should be able to:

- Understand the concept and importance of **unit testing** in C++.
- Write unit tests using frameworks like **Google Test** and **Catch2**.
- Follow the **Test-Driven Development (TDD)** process to build features incrementally.
- Implement unit tests for classes, including those that interact with external resources like files.

In the next chapter, we will explore **advanced testing techniques**, such as **mocking**, **integration testing**, and **performance testing**.

CHAPTER 24

OPTIMIZING C++ CODE FOR PERFORMANCE

Understanding Time Complexity and Big-O Notation

When writing C++ code, **performance** is often a critical consideration. Understanding how your code scales as the size of the input grows is key to writing efficient programs. This is where **time complexity** and **Big-O notation** come into play.

Time Complexity:

Time complexity describes how the runtime of an algorithm changes as the size of the input grows. It helps you understand how efficient your algorithm is. The time complexity is typically measured in terms of the **number of operations** an algorithm performs relative to the size of the input.

Big-O Notation:

Big-O notation is a mathematical notation that describes the upper bound (worst-case scenario) of an algorithm's time complexity. It provides an upper limit on the performance of the algorithm, allowing developers to compare the efficiency of different algorithms.

- **O(1)**: Constant time. The algorithm takes the same amount of time regardless of the size of the input.
- **O(log n)**: Logarithmic time. The algorithm's time grows logarithmically as the input size increases (common in algorithms like binary search).
- **O(n)**: Linear time. The time grows linearly with the size of the input (e.g., iterating through an array).
- **O(n log n)**: Linearithmic time. Common in efficient sorting algorithms like **Merge Sort** and **Quick Sort**.
- **O(n²)**: Quadratic time. The time grows quadratically with the input size (common in algorithms like **Bubble Sort** and **Insertion Sort**).
- **O(2^n)**: Exponential time. The time doubles with each additional element, which is highly inefficient for large inputs (e.g., some recursive algorithms like the naïve Fibonacci sequence).
- **O(n!)**: Factorial time. The time grows extremely fast as the input size increases (e.g., the **Travelling Salesman Problem**).

Example: Consider an array with n elements, and you want to find a particular element.

- **Linear Search (O(n))**: In the worst case, you have to check every element in the array to find the target element.
- **Binary Search (O(log n))**: If the array is sorted, you can repeatedly divide the search space in half, reducing the number of checks required.

Understanding time complexity helps in selecting the most appropriate algorithm for your needs, particularly when dealing with large datasets or time-critical applications.

Optimizing Memory Usage and CPU Efficiency

Optimizing memory usage and CPU efficiency ensures that your program runs fast and does not consume unnecessary resources, which is critical for applications running on limited hardware (e.g., embedded systems, mobile apps) or large-scale systems (e.g., web servers, databases).

Memory Optimization:

1. **Avoid Memory Leaks**: Ensure that dynamically allocated memory is properly freed when it is no longer needed. Use **smart pointers** (like `std::unique_ptr`

and `std::shared_ptr`) to automate memory management and avoid leaks.

2. **Minimize Memory Allocations**: Frequent memory allocations can be costly. Use data structures that minimize allocation overhead, such as **std::vector** (which resizes efficiently) and **std::array** (for fixed-size data).

3. **Efficient Data Structures**: Choosing the right data structure can help optimize memory usage. For example:

   o Use **hash maps** (e.g., `std::unordered_map`) for fast lookups instead of arrays when the keys are sparse.

   o Use **compressed data structures** (e.g., **Bloom Filters**) for large datasets with space constraints.

4. **Memory Pooling**: Use custom memory allocators or memory pooling to manage memory allocation in performance-critical sections, reducing overhead from frequent allocations.

CPU Efficiency:

1. **Efficient Algorithms**: As discussed, choosing algorithms with better time complexity (e.g., **O(log n)** instead of **O(n)**) can drastically improve CPU efficiency.

2. **Avoid Redundant Computations**: Use techniques like **memoization** (caching the results of expensive function calls) to avoid repeating computations.

3. **Parallelism and Concurrency**: Take advantage of multiple CPU cores by parallelizing tasks using libraries like **OpenMP**, **C++11 threads**, or **Intel TBB (Threading Building Blocks)**.

4. **Avoid Unnecessary Operations**: Be mindful of operations that can be avoided or optimized. For example:
   o Avoid excessive ing of objects. Use **references** or **pointers** where possible.
   o Minimize the use of expensive operations like **sorting** or **searching** unless necessary.

Example of Memory Optimization:

cpp

```cpp
#include <iostream>
#include <vector>

int main() {
    // Avoiding excessive memory allocation
    std::vector<int> data;
    data.reserve(1000000);    //    Pre-allocate
memory for 1 million elements

    for (int i = 0; i < 1000000; ++i) {
        data.push_back(i);    // No reallocation
during this loop
    }
```

```
    // Using data...
    std::cout << "First element: " << data[0] <<
std::endl;
    return 0;
}
```

Explanation:

- By calling `reserve()`, we pre-allocate memory for the vector, avoiding multiple reallocations as elements are added.

Tools for Profiling C++ Code

Profiling tools help identify bottlenecks in your code by measuring how much time your program spends in different functions and how much memory it consumes. Profiling helps optimize the **hot spots** (parts of the code that take up most of the time) and improve the overall performance.

Popular Profiling Tools:

1. **gprof**: A profiler for GNU applications that helps analyze where your program spends most of its time. It works by instrumenting the code to collect data on function call counts and execution times.

o   To use `gprof`, compile the code with `-pg` flag and run it to generate a profile file (`gmon.out`), then analyze the output with `gprof`.

```bash
```

```
g++ -pg -o my_program my_program.cpp
./my_program
gprof ./my_program gmon.out > analysis.txt
```

2. **Valgrind**: A tool for memory analysis that can detect memory leaks, uninitialized memory reads, and memory usage errors. It is useful for ensuring memory is being managed efficiently.

```bash
```

```
valgrind --leak-check=full ./my_program
```

3. **Intel VTune Profiler**: A performance profiler that provides detailed analysis of CPU utilization, memory access patterns, and threading efficiency.

4. **Perf**: A Linux-based profiler that can be used to measure the performance of applications, including CPU usage, cache hits/misses, and function call statistics.

5. **Visual Studio Profiler**: For Windows users, Visual Studio provides built-in profiling tools that integrate seamlessly with the IDE.

Real-World Example: Optimizing a High-Performance Computing Algorithm

Let's optimize a basic **Matrix Multiplication** algorithm, a common task in high-performance computing (HPC), to improve its CPU efficiency.

Naive Matrix Multiplication:

The naive approach to matrix multiplication has $O(n^3)$ time complexity.

cpp

```cpp
#include <iostream>
#include <vector>

using namespace std;

void matrixMultiplyNaive(const vector<vector<int>>& A, const vector<vector<int>>& B, vector<vector<int>>& C)
{
    int n = A.size();
    for (int i = 0; i < n; i++) {
        for (int j = 0; j < n; j++) {
            C[i][j] = 0;
            for (int k = 0; k < n; k++) {
```

```
                    C[i][j] += A[i][k] * B[k][j];
            }
        }
    }
}

int main() {
    int n = 500;
    vector<vector<int>> A(n, vector<int>(n, 1));
    vector<vector<int>> B(n, vector<int>(n, 1));
    vector<vector<int>> C(n, vector<int>(n));

    matrixMultiplyNaive(A, B, C);
    cout << "Matrix multiplication completed." <<
endl;

    return 0;
}
```

Optimized Matrix Multiplication (Blocking and Loop Unrolling):

We can optimize this algorithm using **blocking** (also known as **tiling**), which breaks the matrix into smaller sub-matrices that fit better in the cache, reducing memory access latency.

cpp

```
#include <iostream>
#include <vector>
```

```cpp
using namespace std;

void                     matrixMultiplyOptimized(const
vector<vector<int>>&         A,           const
vector<vector<int>>& B, vector<vector<int>>& C)
{
    int n = A.size();
    int blockSize = 32;  // Block size for cache
optimization

    for (int i = 0; i < n; i += blockSize) {
        for (int j = 0; j < n; j += blockSize) {
            for (int k = 0; k < n; k += blockSize)
{
                for (int ii = i; ii < min(i +
blockSize, n); ++ii) {
                    for (int jj = j; jj < min(j
+ blockSize, n); ++jj) {
                        for (int kk = k; kk <
min(k + blockSize, n); ++kk) {
                            C[ii][jj]            +=
A[ii][kk] * B[kk][jj];
                        }
                    }
                }
            }
        }
    }
}
```

```
int main() {
    int n = 500;
    vector<vector<int>> A(n, vector<int>(n, 1));
    vector<vector<int>> B(n, vector<int>(n, 1));
    vector<vector<int>> C(n, vector<int>(n));

    matrixMultiplyOptimized(A, B, C);
    cout << "Optimized matrix multiplication
completed." << endl;

    return 0;
}
```

Explanation:

- **Blocking**: Divides the matrix into smaller blocks to optimize cache usage, improving performance.
- **Time Complexity**: This optimized algorithm can reduce the time complexity to around $O(n^2 \log n)$ in practical use, thanks to better memory access patterns.

Profiling the Algorithm:

After optimization, use profiling tools like **gprof** or **Valgrind** to compare the performance of the naive and optimized algorithms. You should see a significant improvement in execution time due to cache optimization and reduced memory access overhead.

Summary:

By the end of this chapter, you should:

- Understand **time complexity** and **Big-O notation**, and how to apply them to evaluate the efficiency of algorithms.
- Learn how to optimize **memory usage** and **CPU efficiency** in C++.
- Be familiar with **profiling tools** like **gprof**, **Valgrind**, and **Intel VTune** to analyze and optimize your code.
- Gain hands-on experience with optimizing a **high-performance computing algorithm** like matrix multiplication.

In the next chapter, we will explore **multithreading and concurrency** in C++ to further improve performance in multi-core environments.

CHAPTER 25

C++ IN EMBEDDED SYSTEMS AND IOT

Introduction to Embedded C++ Development

Embedded Systems are specialized computing systems designed to perform a specific function or task. These systems are usually constrained by factors such as power consumption, processing power, and memory. As a result, embedded programming often requires a deep understanding of hardware and software to ensure that the system is efficient and reliable.

Embedded C++ is a variation of C++ that is used in resource-constrained environments. While standard C++ is used for general-purpose software development, **Embedded C++** is tailored for low-level programming on microcontrollers, real-time operating systems (RTOS), and hardware. It includes using optimized libraries, minimizing overhead, and directly interacting with hardware components.

Some key features of embedded C++:

- **Memory and performance optimizations**: Embedded C++ focuses on optimizing memory usage and performance.
- **Hardware control**: Embedded systems often require direct interaction with hardware components, such as sensors, motors, and communication protocols.
- **Real-time constraints**: Many embedded systems have real-time constraints, requiring careful scheduling and prioritization of tasks.

In this chapter, we will explore how to use C++ for **IoT devices** and **embedded systems**, focusing on programming **microcontrollers** like **Arduino** and interfacing with sensors to create simple, real-world applications.

C++ for IoT Devices

The **Internet of Things (IoT)** refers to the network of devices, vehicles, appliances, and sensors that are connected to the internet and can exchange data. C++ is commonly used in IoT devices because of its performance and control over hardware resources. IoT devices often require programming that involves:

- **Low-power consumption**.
- **Efficient memory usage**.
- **Real-time operations**.

Common IoT Devices:

- **Microcontrollers**: These are small, low-cost computing devices used in embedded systems. Examples include the **Arduino, Raspberry Pi**, and **ESP32**.
- **Sensors**: Devices that collect data from the environment, such as temperature, humidity, and motion sensors.
- **Actuators**: Components that take action based on sensor data, such as motors or LEDs.

C++ Libraries for IoT:

- **Arduino C++ Libraries**: Arduino provides a simple interface to write C++ code that interacts with sensors, motors, and communication protocols.
- **MQTT**: A lightweight messaging protocol for small sensors and mobile devices, commonly used in IoT.
- **RTOS (Real-Time Operating Systems)**: For more complex IoT devices, using an RTOS like **FreeRTOS** allows for managing tasks with real-time constraints.

Working with Microcontrollers and Sensors

Microcontrollers:

A **microcontroller** is a small computing device that contains a CPU, memory (RAM and ROM), and input/output peripherals all in one chip. Popular microcontrollers for C++ development include:

- **Arduino**: A popular open-source platform based on microcontrollers, suitable for beginners.
- **ESP32**: A low-power, high-performance microcontroller with built-in Wi-Fi and Bluetooth capabilities, ideal for IoT applications.
- **STM32**: A family of microcontrollers based on ARM Cortex processors, widely used in industrial applications.

Interfacing with Sensors:

C++ allows you to read data from sensors (e.g., temperature, pressure, humidity) and process it for IoT applications. To interact with sensors, you'll need to:

- **Connect the sensor** to the microcontroller using standard communication protocols like **I2C**, **SPI**, or **UART**.
- **Configure the sensor** through its register settings.
- **Read the sensor data** and process it.

Communication Protocols:

- **I2C (Inter-Integrated Circuit)**: A two-wire protocol for communication between devices, commonly used for connecting sensors to microcontrollers.

- **SPI (Serial Peripheral Interface)**: A high-speed protocol for connecting sensors and other devices to a microcontroller.
- **UART (Universal Asynchronous Receiver/Transmitter)**: A simple communication protocol used for serial data transfer.

Real-World Example: Creating a Temperature Monitoring System Using C++ and an Arduino

In this example, we will build a **temperature monitoring system** using an **Arduino** and a **DHT11 temperature and humidity sensor**. The system will read temperature data from the sensor and display it on the Arduino Serial Monitor.

Components Required:

- **Arduino Uno** (or any other Arduino model).
- **DHT11 Temperature and Humidity Sensor**.
- **Breadboard and jumper wires**.

Wiring:

- Connect the **VCC** pin of the DHT11 sensor to the **5V** pin on the Arduino.
- Connect the **GND** pin of the DHT11 sensor to the **GND** pin on the Arduino.

- Connect the **DATA** pin of the DHT11 sensor to a digital I/O pin (e.g., **D2**) on the Arduino.

Arduino Code (C++):

cpp

```cpp
#include <DHT.h>

#define DHTPIN 2        // Pin where the data pin
of the sensor is connected
#define DHTTYPE DHT11    // DHT 11 sensor type

DHT dht(DHTPIN, DHTTYPE);  // Create an instance
of the DHT sensor

void setup() {
  Serial.begin(9600);     // Start the Serial
Monitor
  dht.begin();            // Initialize the DHT
sensor
}

void loop() {
  // Wait a few seconds between measurements
  delay(2000);

  // Read the temperature from the sensor
  float temperature = dht.readTemperature();
```

```
  // Check if the reading is valid
  if (isnan(temperature)) {
    Serial.println("Failed to read temperature
from sensor!");
  } else {
    // Print the temperature to the Serial
Monitor
    Serial.print("Temperature: ");
    Serial.print(temperature);
    Serial.println(" °C");
  }
}
```

Explanation:

- We use the **DHT library** to interact with the **DHT11** sensor.
- The `readTemperature()` function reads the temperature value from the sensor.
- The data is printed to the **Serial Monitor** every 2 seconds.

Step-by-Step Process:

1. **Set up hardware**: Connect the **DHT11 sensor** to the **Arduino** as described.
2. **Upload code to Arduino**: Use the Arduino IDE to upload the provided C++ code to the Arduino board.

3. **Open the Serial Monitor**: After uploading, open the **Serial Monitor** in the Arduino IDE to see the temperature readings printed every 2 seconds.

Extending the Project: Sending Data to an IoT Platform

Once you have the basic temperature monitoring system working, you can extend it by sending the data to an **IoT platform**. This could be as simple as sending the temperature data to a **cloud service** using **MQTT** or **HTTP**.

For example, you could:

- Set up the **ESP32** to read the temperature and send the data over Wi-Fi to a **web server**.
- Use **ThingSpeak** (an IoT platform) to display the temperature data in real-time.

Example: Using ESP32 and MQTT:

1. **Install the MQTT Library**: In the Arduino IDE, go to **Sketch > Include Library > Manage Libraries**, search for **PubSubClient**, and install it.
2. **ESP32 Code** (Sending Data to MQTT Server):

cpp

```cpp
#include <WiFi.h>
#include <PubSubClient.h>

const char* ssid = "your_SSID";
const char* password = "your_PASSWORD";
const char* mqtt_server = "mqtt.example.com";  //
Replace with your MQTT server

WiFiClient espClient;
PubSubClient client(espClient);

void setup() {
  Serial.begin(115200);
  WiFi.begin(ssid, password);

  // Wait for connection
  while (WiFi.status() != WL_CONNECTED) {
    delay(1000);
    Serial.println("Connecting to WiFi...");
  }

  Serial.println("Connected to WiFi");
  client.setServer(mqtt_server, 1883);
}

void loop() {
  if (!client.connected()) {
    reconnect();
  }
```

```cpp
  client.loop();

  // Example: Send temperature data to MQTT
server
  String payload = "Temperature: 25°C";
  client.publish("home/temperature",
payload.c_str());
  delay(5000);  // Send data every 5 seconds
}

void reconnect() {
  // Loop until reconnected
  while (!client.connected()) {
    if (client.connect("ESP32Client")) {
      client.subscribe("home/temperature");
    } else {
      delay(5000);
    }
  }
}
```

This simple extension allows your temperature monitoring system to send data to an **MQTT broker** for remote monitoring.

Summary:

By the end of this chapter, you should:

- Understand how to use **C++ for embedded systems** and **IoT devices**.
- Be familiar with **microcontrollers** like **Arduino** and **ESP32** and how to interface with **sensors**.
- Have created a **temperature monitoring system** using C++ and Arduino, and optionally extended it to send data to an **IoT platform**.
- Gain insight into **IoT communication protocols** like **MQTT** for real-time data transmission.

In the next chapter, we will explore **advanced IoT applications**, such as **sensor networks**, **edge computing**, and integrating with **cloud services**.

CHAPTER 26

ADVANCED C++ BEST PRACTICES

Code Readability and Maintainability

Writing readable and maintainable code is one of the cornerstones of professional software development. In C++, this becomes even more important because of its complexity, power, and features. Following best practices not only ensures that your code works correctly but also that it is understandable to other developers (or even to yourself) in the future.

1. Naming Conventions

- **Variables**: Use descriptive names that clearly indicate the purpose of the variable. For example, instead of `int x`, use `int temperature` or `int userAge`.
- **Functions**: Function names should be verbs and clearly describe the action they perform. For instance, `int calculateArea()` is more descriptive than `int func()`.

- **Classes**: Class names should be nouns, typically in PascalCase. For example, `class Rectangle` or `class Employee`.
- **Constants and Macros**: Constants and macros should be written in uppercase letters, using underscores for separation, e.g., `const int MAX_SIZE = 100`.

2. Consistent Formatting

- **Indentation**: Use consistent indentation (4 spaces per indent is common). This helps to visualize the structure of your code clearly.
- **Braces**: Always use braces { } even for single-line blocks to avoid potential issues in the future. This improves readability and avoids bugs caused by missing braces.

Example:

```cpp
if (condition) {
    // some logic
} else {
    // some logic
}
```

- **Spacing**: Use spaces around operators, after commas, and after keywords for better readability.

Example:

cpp

```cpp
int sum = a + b;
```

3. Commenting

- **Write comments to explain the *why*, not the *what*.** Good code should be self-explanatory, but comments should explain the reasoning behind a decision, particularly if it's non-obvious.

- Use **inline comments** sparingly to clarify specific lines of code.

- For **function comments**, explain what the function does, the parameters it accepts, and what it returns.

Example:

cpp

```cpp
// Calculates the area of a rectangle.
// Parameters: width (int), height (int)
// Returns: area (int)
int calculateArea(int width, int height) {
    return width * height;
}
```

4. Avoiding Code Duplication

- **DRY (Don't Repeat Yourself)**: Repeated code can lead to errors and makes maintenance harder. Abstract common functionality into functions, classes, or templates.
- **Use functions** for repeated logic and **reusable components** to make your code easier to maintain.

Using C++ Libraries Efficiently

C++ offers a vast range of **standard libraries** (STL) and third-party libraries that can help reduce development time and improve the quality of your code. However, it's crucial to use them **efficiently**.

1. Use the Standard Library (STL)

- **Vectors, Sets, Maps**: The STL offers a wide range of containers that are highly optimized. Use them instead of writing your own containers from scratch.
- **Algorithms**: The STL provides numerous algorithms (like `std::sort()`, `std::find()`, `std::accumulate()`) that can simplify your code and improve efficiency.

    Example:

```
cpp

#include <vector>
#include <algorithm>

std::vector<int> nums = {5, 2, 8, 3, 1};
std::sort(nums.begin(), nums.end());   //
Sorting the vector using STL sort
```

2. Use Smart Pointers

- Instead of manually managing memory with `new` and `delete`, use **smart pointers** (`std::unique_ptr`, `std::shared_ptr`) to manage memory automatically and reduce memory leaks.

Example:

```
cpp

std::unique_ptr<int>        ptr        =
std::make_unique<int>(5);
// Automatically deleted when it goes out
of scope
```

3. Avoid Premature Optimization

- While libraries like **Boost** or **Eigen** are powerful, don't use them prematurely unless they provide significant performance benefits. Start with simpler solutions and optimize only when performance bottlenecks are identified.

4. Third-Party Libraries

- Utilize libraries that offer ready-to-use solutions. For example:
    - o **Boost**: A collection of highly regarded libraries that extend the functionality of the C++ Standard Library.
    - o **OpenCV**: For computer vision tasks.
    - o **Qt**: For creating cross-platform applications with GUIs.

Handling Complex Software Projects in C++

When working on complex software projects, it's essential to organize your code efficiently, adhere to best practices, and use the right tools to ensure success. Here are some best practices for managing large C++ projects:

1. Modularization

- Break your project into smaller, manageable modules or components. This makes the code easier to maintain and test.

- Each **module** should have a clear responsibility and should interact with other modules through well-defined interfaces.

Example:

cpp

```cpp
// In file Rectangle.h
class Rectangle {
public:
    int width;
    int height;
    int calculateArea();
};

// In file Rectangle.cpp
#include "Rectangle.h"
int Rectangle::calculateArea() {
    return width * height;
}
```

2. Use of Header Files and Implementations

- Keep declarations in **header files** (.h or .hpp), and **implementations** in .cpp files. This improves code organization and reduces compile-time dependencies.

3. Dependency Management

- For large projects, use build systems like **CMake**, **Makefile**, or **Premake** to manage dependencies and automate the compilation process.
- Use **package managers** (like **Conan** or **vcpkg**) to manage third-party libraries and keep track of dependencies.

4. Unit Testing and Continuous Integration (CI)

- Implement **unit tests** to ensure code correctness and refactorability. Tools like **Google Test** or **Catch2** help automate testing.
- Use **continuous integration** services (such as **Travis CI**, **GitHub Actions**, or **Jenkins**) to automatically test your code whenever changes are made.

Real-World Example: Building a C++ Plugin System for a Media Player

In this example, we will build a **plugin system** for a simple media player. This system will allow the media player to load and utilize plugins at runtime, making it extensible.

Step 1: Define the Plugin Interface

The **plugin interface** defines the functionality that plugins must implement. We'll create a base class `Plugin` that all plugins must inherit from.

cpp

```cpp
// Plugin.h
class Plugin {
public:
    virtual void execute() = 0;  // Pure virtual function
    virtual ~Plugin() = default;
};
```

Step 2: Implement a Media Player Plugin

Now, we'll implement a plugin for our media player. For simplicity, let's create a `PlayMusicPlugin` that simulates playing music.

cpp

```cpp
// PlayMusicPlugin.h
#include "Plugin.h"
#include <iostream>

class PlayMusicPlugin : public Plugin {
public:
```

```cpp
    void execute() override {
        std::cout << "Playing music..." <<
std::endl;
    }
};
```

Step 3: Load Plugins Dynamically

To allow the media player to load plugins at runtime, we will use **dynamic linking** via shared libraries.

cpp

```cpp
// MediaPlayer.cpp
#include <iostream>
#include <memory>
#include <dlfcn.h>    // For dynamic loading
(Linux)

// Function to load a plugin
std::unique_ptr<Plugin>          loadPlugin(const
std::string& pluginPath) {
    void*            pluginHandle          =
dlopen(pluginPath.c_str(), RTLD_LAZY);
    if (!pluginHandle) {
        std::cerr << "Error loading plugin: " <<
dlerror() << std::endl;
        return nullptr;
    }
```

```
    auto       createPlugin      =        (Plugin*
(*)())dlsym(pluginHandle, "createPlugin");
    if (!createPlugin) {
        std::cerr << "Error finding function: "
<< dlerror() << std::endl;
        return nullptr;
    }

    return
std::unique_ptr<Plugin>(createPlugin());
}

int main() {
    // Example of loading a plugin dynamically
    auto            plugin            =
loadPlugin("./PlayMusicPlugin.so");
    if (plugin) {
        plugin->execute();  // Call the plugin's
execute method
    }
    return 0;
}
```

Step 4: Compile and Link

- **Compile the Media Player**: Use g++ or another C++ compiler to compile the media player code.
- **Create the Plugin**: Compile the plugin as a shared library (e.g., PlayMusicPlugin.so).

```
bash

g++      -shared      -o      PlayMusicPlugin.so
PlayMusicPlugin.cpp -fPIC
g++ -o MediaPlayer MediaPlayer.cpp -ldl
```

Step 5: Running the Media Player

When you run the media player, it will dynamically load the `PlayMusicPlugin.so` and execute the plugin's functionality, simulating playing music.

Summary:

By the end of this chapter, you should:

- Understand the importance of **code readability** and **maintainability** in C++.
- Be familiar with **best practices** for **using C++ libraries**, **modularizing your code**, and **managing dependencies**.
- Know how to handle **complex software projects** in C++, including **unit testing** and **continuous integration**.
- Have implemented a **real-world example** of a **plugin system** for a media player in C++.

In the next chapter, we will explore **advanced C++ techniques** such as **multi-threading**, **parallel programming**, and **optimizing performance** in real-time applications.

CHAPTER 27

FUTURE OF C++ AND CONCLUSION

Trends and Innovations in C++ Development

C++ has been a cornerstone of software development for decades, and despite the rise of newer programming languages, it remains a dominant force in industries where performance and control are critical. The future of C++ is marked by continuous evolution, with several **trends** and **innovations** emerging to make it more powerful, versatile, and easier to use.

1. C++20 and Beyond

C++ has been evolving with the release of new standards like **C++11**, **C++14**, **C++17**, and **C++20**, each adding new features and optimizations. The **C++20** standard introduced several key features:

- **Concepts**: A type system feature that provides better constraints on templates, improving code readability and error messages.

- **Ranges**: A powerful set of tools for working with sequences of data in a more functional style, reducing boilerplate code.
- **Coroutines**: A feature that simplifies asynchronous programming, enabling easier handling of tasks like I/O operations, concurrent execution, and more.
- **Modules**: These reduce compilation times and improve the organization of code by providing a more efficient way to manage dependencies.
- **Calendar and Timezone Libraries**: The `<chrono>` library saw significant updates in C++20, adding a more robust set of features for date and time handling.

2. Enhanced Performance and Optimization

C++ continues to focus on performance improvements. With the rise of **multi-core processors**, C++'s capabilities for **parallel programming** and **multi-threading** are becoming more important. Tools like **OpenMP, C++ standard threads**, and **Intel TBB (Threading Building Blocks)** are being integrated to leverage multi-core processing power, enabling C++ developers to build applications that fully utilize modern hardware.

3. Cross-Platform Development

C++ has become a key language in **cross-platform** development, with libraries and frameworks like **Qt, CMake**, and **Boost** providing robust solutions for writing code that runs on multiple operating systems. **C++ for mobile development** is also growing, with tools like **Cocos2d-x** and **Unreal Engine** enabling the development of games and apps for Android and iOS.

4. Emphasis on Simplicity and Safety

Recent trends in C++ development also focus on making the language safer and easier to use. Features like **smart pointers** (`std::unique_ptr`, `std::shared_ptr`), **RAII (Resource Acquisition Is Initialization)**, and **exception safety** are pushing for more secure and less error-prone coding practices. In addition, **type safety** features such as **Concepts** and **constexpr** are making C++ more robust, reducing the likelihood of bugs and making the language more approachable for new developers.

How C++ is Evolving in Modern Tech

C++ remains relevant in many fields and continues to evolve to meet the demands of modern technology. Let's look at how C++ is playing a vital role in several emerging fields:

1. Artificial Intelligence (AI) and Machine Learning

While languages like **Python** are the go-to choices for machine learning and AI, C++ still plays a critical role in AI applications

322

that demand high performance and low latency, such as **real-time inference systems** and **training large models**.

- **TensorFlow** and **PyTorch**, two of the most widely used AI frameworks, are written in **C++** for performance-critical operations, while their Python APIs offer ease of use for developers.
- **CUDA**: Nvidia's GPU programming model, based on C++, is extensively used for accelerating AI tasks, such as deep learning, on powerful GPUs.

2. Blockchain Development

C++ is one of the most commonly used languages in blockchain technology, particularly for building **cryptocurrency** systems and decentralized applications (dApps). The **Bitcoin** blockchain and **Ethereum** (in its earlier iterations) are both written in C++, leveraging its speed and low-level system capabilities.

- **Blockchain's Need for Speed**: Blockchain operations, such as mining, transactions, and consensus algorithms, require high throughput, low latency, and efficient memory management, making C++ a natural choice.
- **Cryptographic Libraries**: Many cryptographic algorithms, such as those used in **Elliptic Curve Digital Signature Algorithm (ECDSA)**, are optimized using C++ for maximum efficiency.

3. High-Performance Computing (HPC)

C++ has long been the language of choice for **high-performance computing** (HPC) applications that require heavy numerical computations, simulations, and data analysis. It is widely used in areas like:

- **Scientific simulations** (e.g., weather modeling, physics simulations, molecular dynamics).
- **Financial modeling** (e.g., options pricing, risk analysis).
- **Engineering applications** (e.g., computer-aided design, mechanical simulations).
- **HPC Frameworks** like **OpenMP**, **MPI (Message Passing Interface)**, and **CUDA** often use C++ for the computationally intensive components, allowing it to harness modern CPU and GPU architectures for extreme performance.

4. Real-Time Systems

C++ continues to be the dominant language for real-time systems due to its **predictable performance** and ability to interact closely with hardware. This is especially true in **embedded systems** and **automotive applications**, where real-time processing and low-latency responses are essential.

- **Automotive Industry**: Many **autonomous driving systems** are built using C++ for their performance and reliability.
- **Industrial Control Systems**: C++ is used in systems requiring fast, reliable control of manufacturing or robotics processes.

Final Words and Tips for Mastery

Mastering C++ can be a rewarding journey, but it requires dedication, patience, and consistent practice. Here are some key tips for mastering C++:

1. Understand the Fundamentals:

Before diving into advanced topics, ensure you have a solid understanding of **C++ fundamentals**:

- Object-Oriented Programming (OOP): Classes, inheritance, polymorphism.
- Memory management: Pointers, smart pointers, RAII, and manual memory management.
- Templates: Templates and **STL** (Standard Template Library) for reusable and efficient code.

2. Embrace Modern C++:

Stay updated with the latest standards of C++ (C++11, C++14, C++17, C++20). Modern C++ introduces powerful features such as **smart pointers**, **lambda expressions**, **auto keyword**, **range-based loops**, and **constexpr**.

3. Practice Problem Solving:

To sharpen your skills, solve problems on platforms like **LeetCode**, **HackerRank**, or **Codeforces**. Practicing algorithmic challenges will deepen your understanding of data structures, algorithms, and C++ language features.

4. Explore the Ecosystem:

C++ has a rich ecosystem of libraries and tools. Get familiar with widely used libraries such as **Boost**, **Eigen**, and **Qt**. Explore frameworks for game development (**Unreal Engine, SFML, SDL**) and IoT development (**Arduino, Raspberry Pi**).

5. Work on Real-World Projects:

Nothing beats hands-on experience. Build projects such as game engines, IoT devices, blockchain applications, or even a custom web server to put your skills into practice.

6. Read C++ Books and Documentation:

In addition to practical coding, read books like **Effective C++ by Scott Meyers, C++ Primer** by Stanley B. Lippman, and explore the **ISO C++ documentation** to understand the deeper nuances of the language.

Real-World Example: C++'s Role in AI, Blockchain, and High-Performance Computing

Let's discuss how C++ is applied in three real-world, high-impact domains:

1. AI in C++:

C++ is used in AI for performance-critical tasks such as training deep learning models. Libraries like **TensorFlow** and **PyTorch** use C++ for low-level operations such as matrix multiplication and convolution, ensuring that operations can be carried out on powerful hardware like **GPUs**.

For instance, C++ is crucial for:

- **Training AI models**: Handling large datasets and complex algorithms efficiently.
- **Inference**: Once a model is trained, it can be used for real-time predictions on new data, where speed is critical.

327

2. Blockchain in C++:

Blockchain technology benefits from C++'s low-level control over memory and performance. For example, **Bitcoin**'s core implementation uses C++ for the underlying architecture. The protocol's cryptographic functions (hashing, consensus) are implemented in C++, ensuring the platform's high throughput and low-latency transaction processing.

C++ is used for:

- **Cryptographic Algorithms**: Implementing efficient and secure cryptographic functions like **SHA-256** (Bitcoin's hashing algorithm).
- **Transaction Processing**: Ensuring fast and reliable transaction handling in decentralized networks.

3. High-Performance Computing (HPC) in C++:

C++ is the go-to language for **scientific simulations**, **data processing**, and **performance-critical applications**. Its ability to interact with low-level hardware makes it perfect for systems requiring intense computation, such as:

- **Weather Modeling**: C++ models complex physical systems like weather patterns in real-time.

- **Molecular Dynamics**: Simulating interactions between molecules, commonly used in fields like biology and chemistry.

C++ is favored for:

- **Parallel Processing**: Using technologies like **CUDA** and **OpenMP**, C++ can take full advantage of **multi-core** processors and **GPUs** to speed up simulations.

Summary:

By the end of this chapter, you should have:

- A solid understanding of **C++'s future** and its relevance in **modern technology**.
- Knowledge of the **trends and innovations** in C++ development, such as **C++20**, **real-time systems**, and **multi-core processing**.
- Insights into **C++'s role in AI, blockchain**, and **high-performance computing**.
- Tips and strategies for mastering C++ and excelling as a C++ developer.

As C++ continues to evolve, it remains one of the most powerful and versatile programming languages. Embrace its features, stay updated with the latest standards, and continue building projects that push the boundaries of what you can achieve with C++.